Text: JOSEP MARIA CARANDELL Photos: PERE VIVAS

THE TEMPLE OF THE

Sagrada Família

TRIANGLE POSTALS

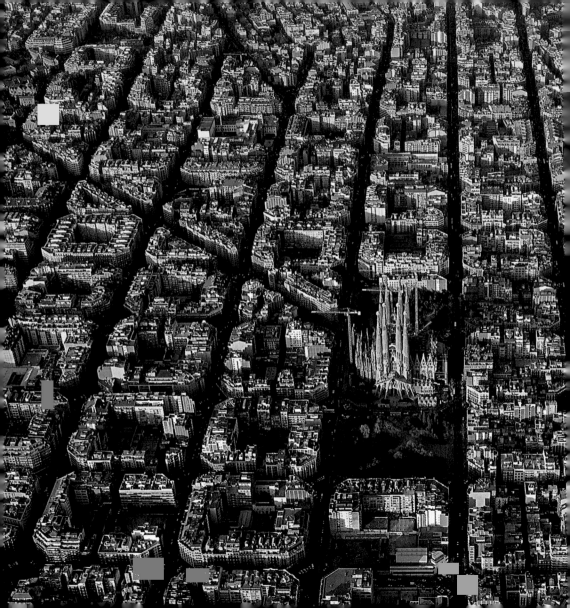

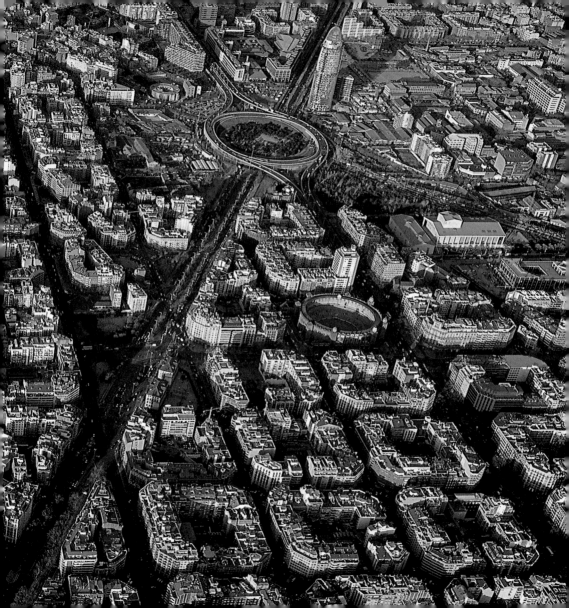

Contents

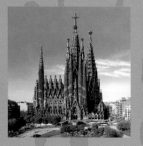 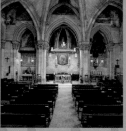 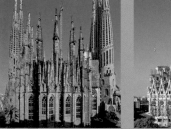 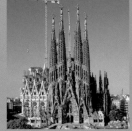

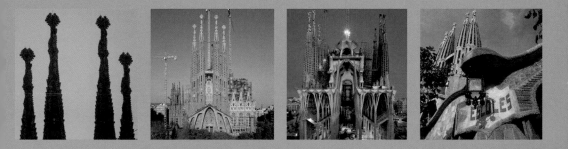

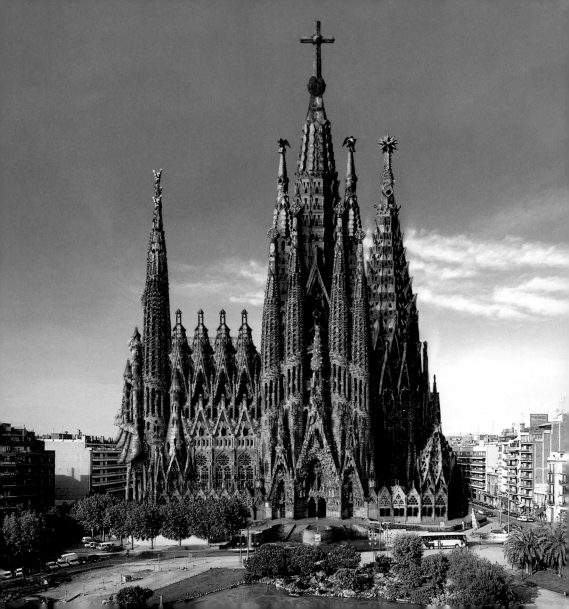

The Third Cathedral

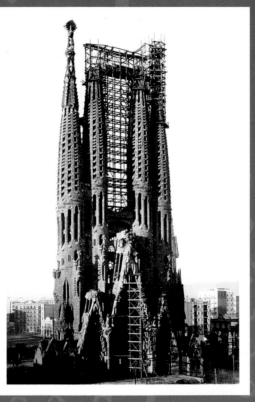

THE FIRST TOWER, DEDICATED TO SAINT
BARNABUS, WAS FINISHED IN 1925

←

PHOTOMONTAGE OF THE FINISHED TEMPLE

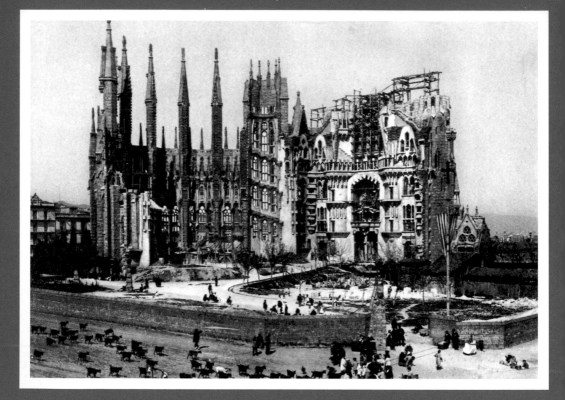

IMAGE OF THE INSIDE OF THE TEMPLE AROUND 1904. THE PHOTOGRAPH CLEARLY SHOWS THE AREA AROUND THE SAGRADA FAMILIA WAS NOT VERY DEVELOPED WITH HERDS OF GOATS STILL WANDERING AROUND

The Third Cathedral

Until the middle of the 19th century, Barcelona was an ancient walled city situated on a narrow coastal plain. Behind it were wide open spaces, protected by a low range, where building was forbidden for reasons of military defence. It was in this area where, from 1860 onwards, construction of the *Eixample* began, a new rectangular-shaped neighbourhood with broad modern streets.

The bookshop owner Josep Mª Bocabella, president of the Association of Devotees of Saint Joseph, would have preferred a site in the middle of the Eixample for the church he had long wanted to build and dedicate to the Holy Family. But the best sites were already highly priced and he had to settle for a location within the rectangle, but in the Poblet district known as Sant Martí

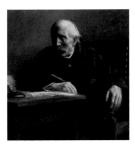

J. M. BOCABELLA (1815-1892)

de Provençals. The latter was a locality where traditional market gardens rubbed shoulders with a cluster of working-class housing for textile industry employees. The advantage was that the land was very much cheaper, so he was able to buy a much bigger site for the price of a whole block in the Ensanche district: 170,000 pesetas which had been collected from all the contributions.

Architectural plans for the new church were needed, and for these Bocabella approached the parish architect Francisco de Villar. The latter planned a Gothic-style building and work was begun on the crypt, but bitter quarrels with Bocabella led him to resign. Months later, in 1883, the young architect Antoni Gaudí, born in Reus in 1852, took his place.

Gaudí, the famous name behind great architectural works such as the Palau Güell and the Batlló and Milà buildings, now had the Sagrada Familia as his life's work –comparable to Goethe and his *Faust*– and to this he dedicated himself until his death, forty-three years later, when he was run over by a tram on leaving the building site.

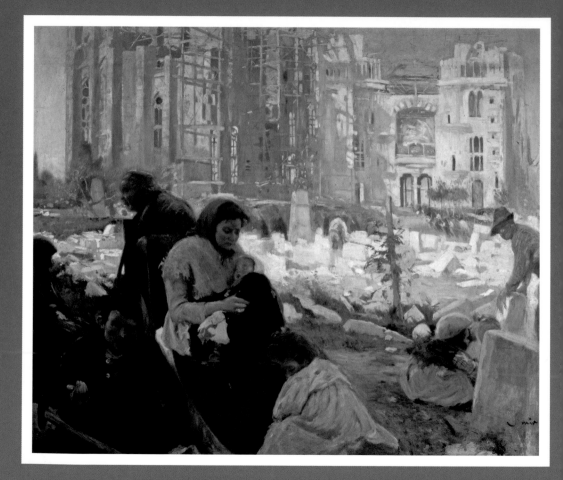

JOAQUIM MIR. "THE CATHEDRAL OF THE POOR", 1898

The Barcelona landmark grew under his direction to such dimensions, taking on such gigantic exuberance and meaning, that it was soon being called a cathedral, in more or less explicit competition with the very See of the Bishop of Barcelona, dating from the 2nd century, whose cathedral in the old city was begun in the 13th century.

Furthermore, since ambitious Barcelona had another medieval church, Santa Maria del Mar, built by the powerful merchants and shipowners, which was proudly referred to as the Cathedral of the Sea, the Sagrada Familia came to be known as Barcelona's third cathedral. A painting by Joaquín Mir, dated 1897, with the Sagrada Familia in the background, is entitled "The Cathedral of the Poor". Gaudí himself regularly referred to the church as the "cathedral", despite the fact that there was no cathedra or see. However, ambitious and brilliant architect as he was, he felt sure that with time, as the poet Maragall put it, Barcelona would be renowned for "his" church, for this cathedral.

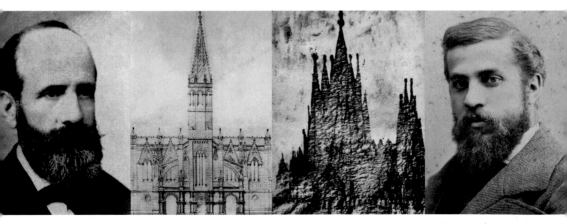

FRANCISCO DE PAULA DEL VILLAR (1828-1901) | PROJECT BY DEL VILLAR (1882) | PROJECT BY GAUDÍ | GAUDÍ ON FINISHING HIS STUDIES (1878)

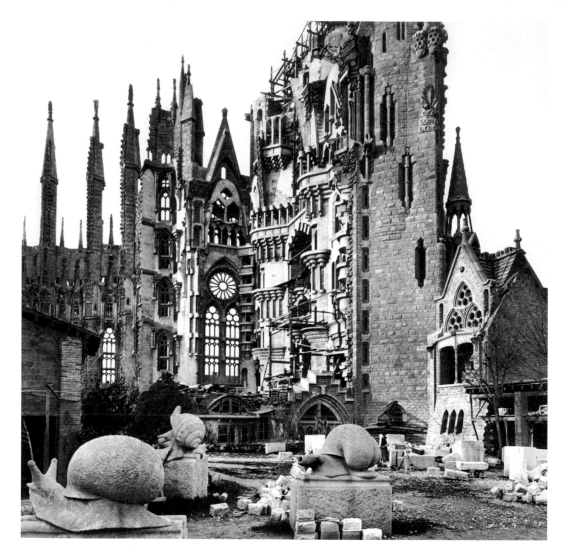

IN GOTHIC CATHEDRALS THE GARGOYLES ARE GIVEN THE FORM OF FANTASTIC BEINGS, BUT IN THE SAGRADA FAMILIA THESE ELEMENTS ARE INSPIRED BY NATURE, JUST AS CAN BE SEEN IN THESE SNAILS-GARGOYLES SCULPTED BY LLORENÇ MATAMALA FROM NATURALLY CAST MOULDS

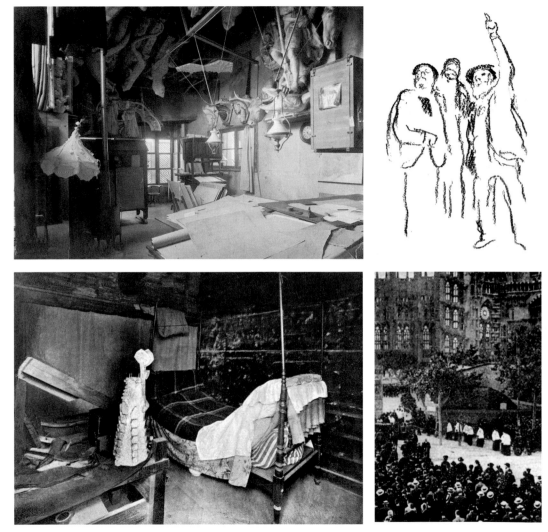

GAUDÍ'S STUDY AND BEDROOM IN THE TEMPLE | GAUDÍ SHOWING THE TEMPLE IN A DRAWING BY OPISSO | THE ARCHITECT'S FUNERAL (1926)

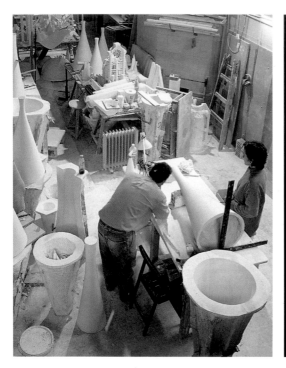

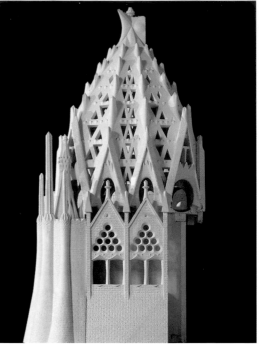

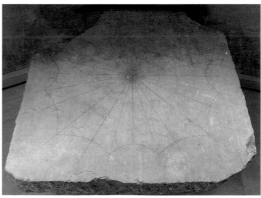

MODEL WORKSHOP

GAUDÍ LEFT MODELS OF THE UNBUILT PARTS OF THE TEMPLE.
THE MODEL OF THE SACRISTY ROOFING HAS BEEN OF SPECIAL
IMPORTANCE. ITS GEOMETRY, IN WHICH THE USE OF NEW
TECHNOLOGIES IN INTERPRETING IT HAS BEEN DETERMINANT,
WILL PROVIDE THE FORM OF THE MOST IMPORTANT TOWERS
OF THE CATHEDRAL DEDICATED TO JESUS AND MARY

GAUDÍ WORKED IN THE SAGRADA FAMILIA FOLLOWING THE
EXAMPLE OF THE OLD CRAFTSMEN'S GUILDS. PROOF OF HIS
LOYALTY TO TRADITION IS THE DRAWING OF THE GROUND
PLAN OF THE SACRISTY MADE OVER THE SURFACE OF A
STONE, A WIDESPREAD HABIT AMONGST THE CATHEDRAL
BUILDERS OF THE PAST

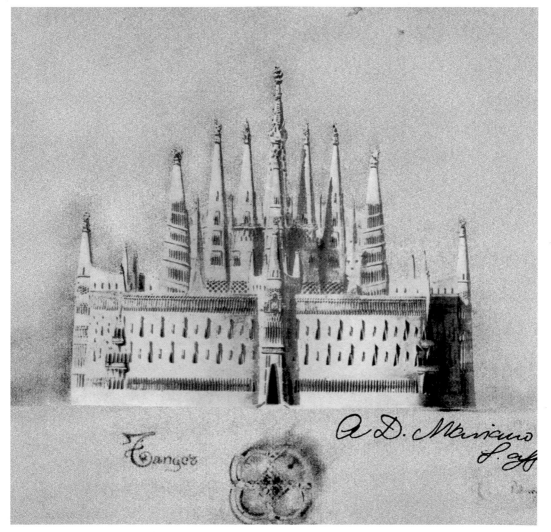

THE PROJECT THAT WAS NOT UNDERTAKEN FOR THE CATHOLIC MISSIONS OF TANGIER (1893) CONTAINS
IN ESSENCE THE MORPHOLOGY OF THE TOWERS DEVELOPED BY GAUDÍ IN THE SAGRADA FAMILIA

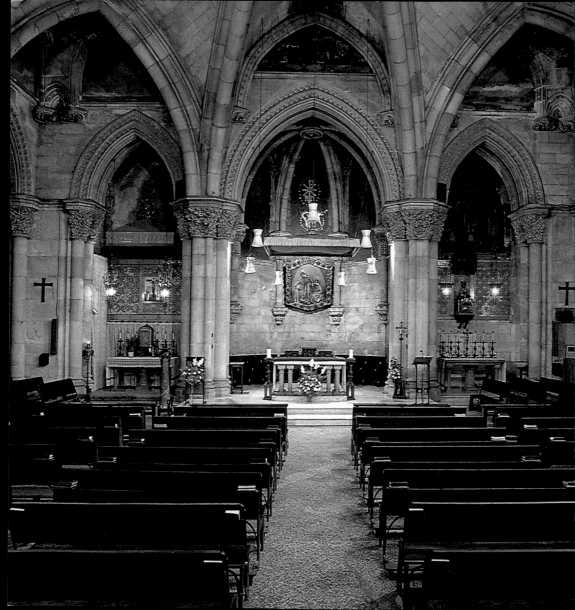

The Crypt

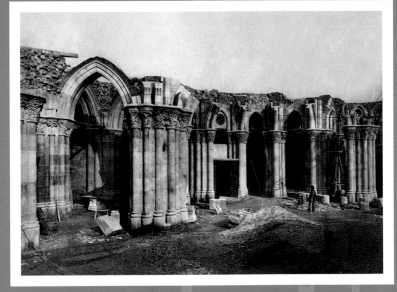

IN 1883, GAUDÍ REPLACED FRANCISCO DEL VILLAR AS HEAD OF WORKS OF THE TEMPLE AND CONTINUED HIS CONSTRUCTION OF THE ALREADY-BEGUN CRYPT. THIS PHOTOGRAPH, PUBLISHED IN 1886 IN "EL PROPAGADOR DE SAN JOSÉ", SHOWS GAUDÍ'S LOYALTY TO THE NEO-GOTHIC STYLE PROPOSED BY HIS PREDECESSOR

←
THE CENTRAL ALTAR

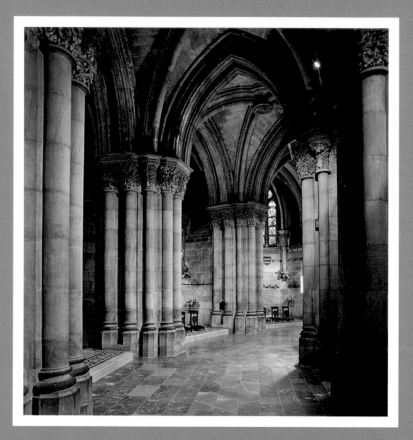

AMBULATORY OF THE CRYPT

The Crypt

Dug out of the subsoil, between the Nativity and Passion entrances, lies the crypt. In Greek, crypt means "hidden place", and recalls the primitive Christian burial places concealed under houses and in catacombs in times of persecution.

In 1882, the construction of the church began with the crypt, at the instance of the Association of Devotees of Saint Joseph, with F. del Villar in charge. A year later del Villar was replaced by the thirty-one year old Gaudí, a man who had completed few buildings, but who was ambitious and already well-known for his energy and originality, as well as being a protégé of the influential Comillas and Güell families. Gaudí would have preferred having the Nativity façade of the building orientated towards the rising sun, and the Passion and Death façade facing the setting sun, as was traditionally done. However, the crypt (already begun by del Villar) impeded him, so the orientation had to be somewhat rotated. His own contribution was to construct the domed vault of the crypt and surround it by a dry moat, so that it would receive light and air directly. This was completed in 1891.

The crypt, in neo-gothic style like most religious buildings of the 19th century, took the form of a rotunda with seven chapels –the middle one dedicated to Saint Joseph, who had recently been named patron saint of the Catholic Church– facing five chapels. The middle one of the latter had the altar for the celebration of Mass, as well as a bas-relief of the Holy Family in their house in Nazareth, by Josep Llimona. The emphasis on the Holy Family, consisting of Jesus, Mary and Joseph, derives from the shrine at Loreto in Italy, to where, according to tradition, the angels spirited the house where Jesus had been conceived. To the left are the chapel of the Virgin of Montserrat, Catalonia's patron saint, and the chapel of Holy Christ, at whose feet Joseph Maria Bocabella, founder of the Josephine order, is buried. To the right are the chapels of the Holy Sacrament and Our Lady of Carmen. Gaudí was much devoted to the latter Virgin, and wished to be buried at her feet, where the stone reads: "Antonius Gaudí Cornet, reusensis".

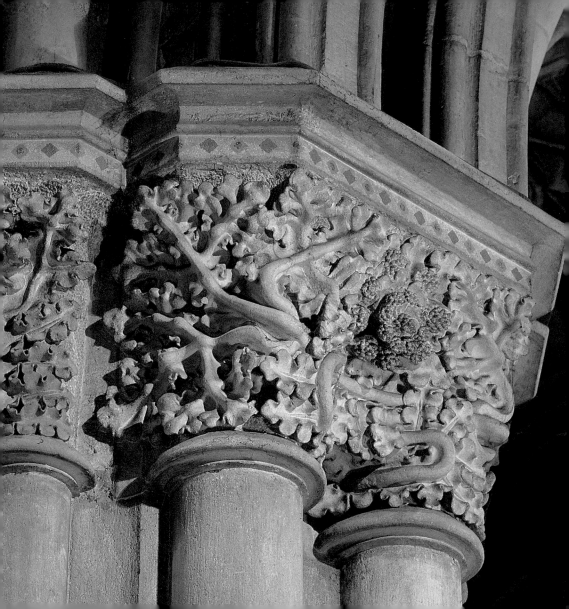

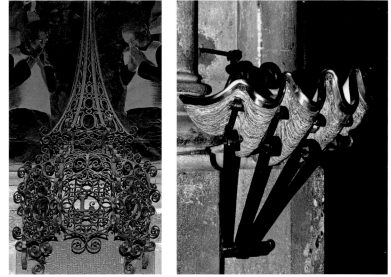

CAPITALS WITH BOTANICAL MOTIFS

—

WROUGHT-IRON DECORATION
OF THE CHAPEL OF THE VIRGIN
OF MONTSERRAT

EUSEBI GÜELL GAVE GAUDÍ
ENORMOUS SHELLS FROM THE
PHILIPPINES. ONE OF THEM
WAS USED IN THE CRYPT AS
A HOLY WATER STOUP

The Chapel of Saint Joseph is flanked by the Chapel of the Immaculate Conception, whose doctrine of virginity had been joyfully and clamorously celebrated by Catholics. Next to it is the Chapel of the Sacred Heart, where Jesus' heart represents the most human aspect of the Son of God. The remaining chapels will be dedicated to members of Jesus' family and sacristies. The angels supporting the columns on their heads –with two, four or six wings– are inspired by the book of Revelations.

The central plaque in the vault is essential, not just as the confluence of the main arches, but also because it features the multicoloured work by Flotats depicting the Annunciation and Incarnation –a mystery that relates together all the figures in the Crypt, as well as all the cathedral, and indeed, the whole of the Catholic church.

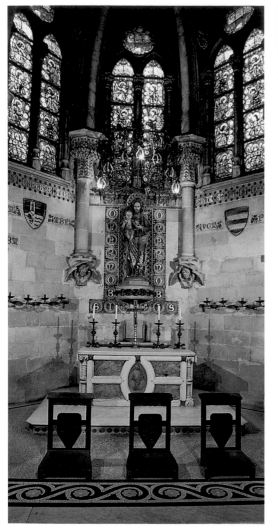 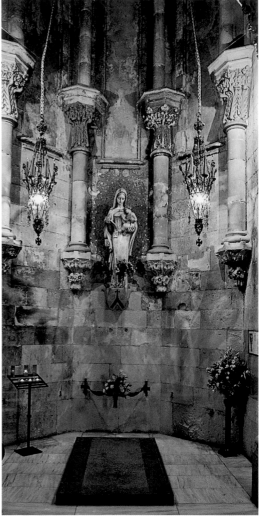

THE CHAPEL OF SAINT JOSEPH AND OUR LADY OF CARMEN, WITH GAUDÍ'S TOMB | POINTED ARCHES OF THE AMBULATORY

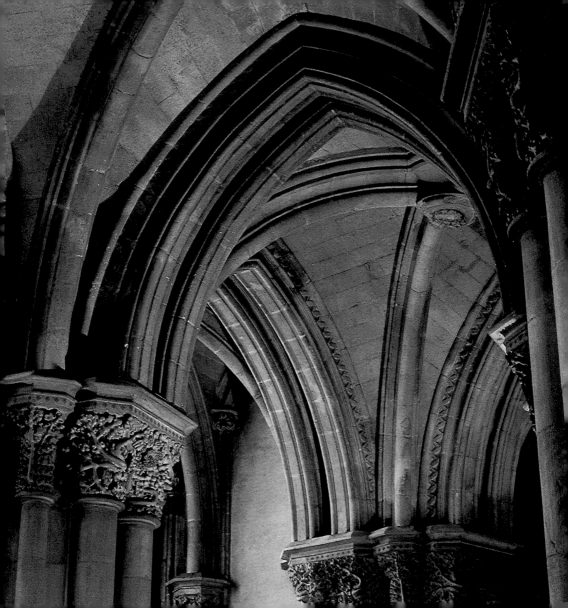

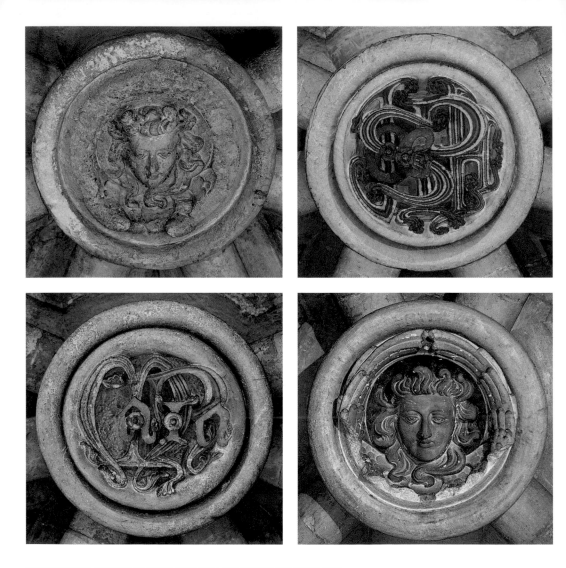

KEYSTONES IN THE CRYPT VAULTING WITH ANGELS AND ANAGRAMS OF JOSEPH AND MARY

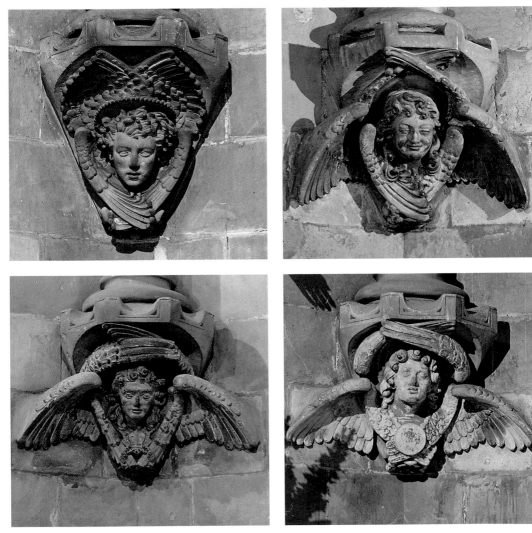

TWO, FOUR AND SIX-WINGED ANGELS, REPRESENTING THOSE MENTIONED IN THE APOCALYPSE, HOLDING UP COLUMNS

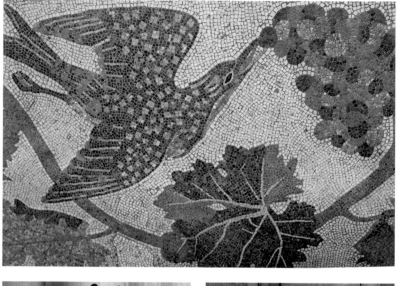

ROMAN MOSAIC IN THE CRYPT FLOOR DESIGNED BY GAUDÍ AND PRODUCED BY MARIO MARAGLIANO

FOUR-ARMED EASTER CANDLE THAT OPENS OUT IN THE FORM OF A CROSS AND ENABLES THE CANDLESTICK TO BE SEPARATED FROM THE WOODEN SHAFT SO THAT IT CAN BE CARRIED ON THE EASTER SATURDAY PROCESSION (C. 1898)

WOODEN CONFESSIONAL BOX BUILT AROUND 1898 IN THE WORKSHOP OF JOAN MUNNÉ

—

LAMPS FROM THE ALTAR OF THE SACRED HEART AND THE ALTAR OF THE VIRGIN (C. 1923-1926)

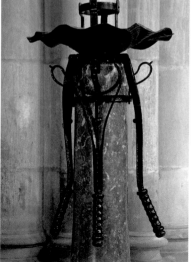

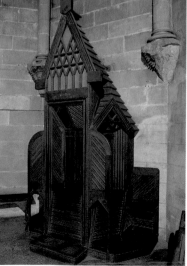

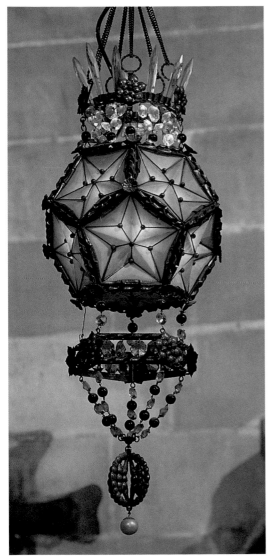

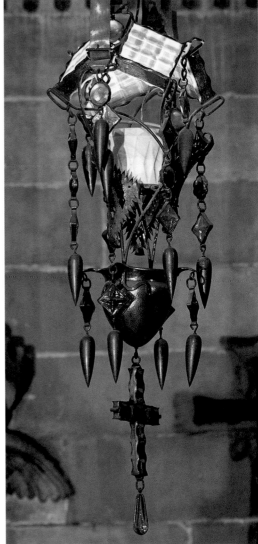

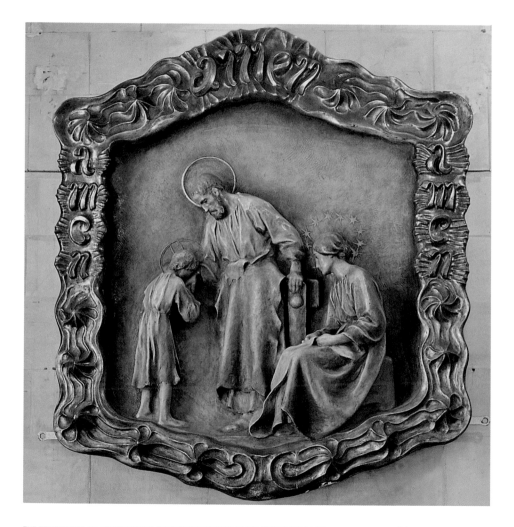

THE RELIEF WORK BY JOSEP LLIMONA DEDICATED TO THE SAGRADA FAMILIA COMES FROM THE CASA BATLLÓ | CENTRAL
KEYSTONE OF THE CRYPT WITH THE ANNUNCIATION, THE INCARNATION OF THE WORD, A PIECE OF WORK BY JOAN FLOTATS

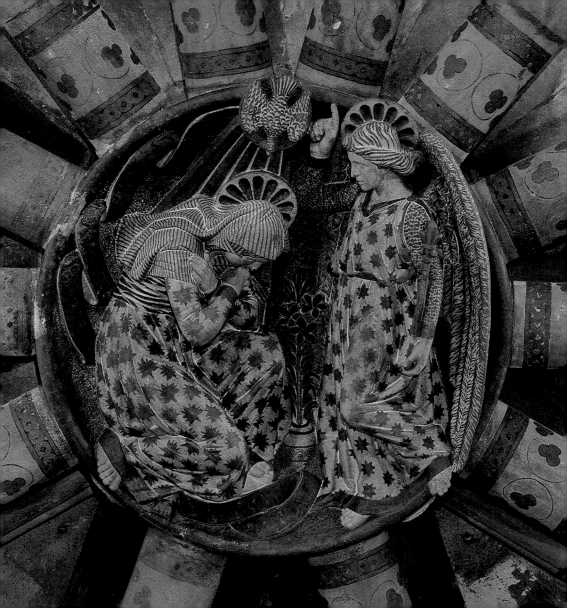

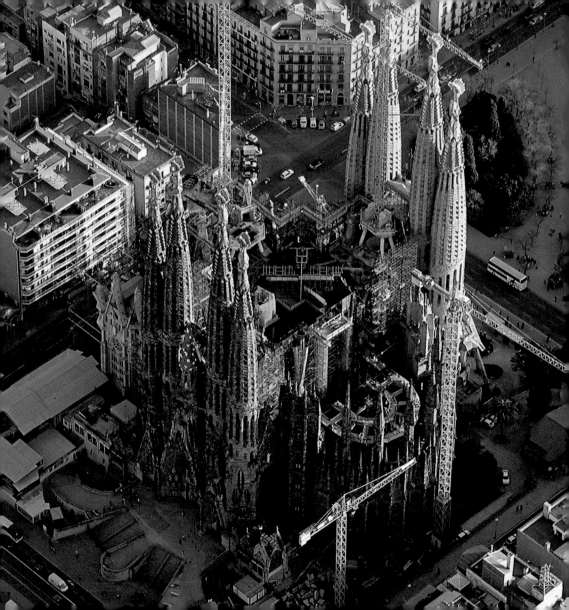

The Apse and the Cloister

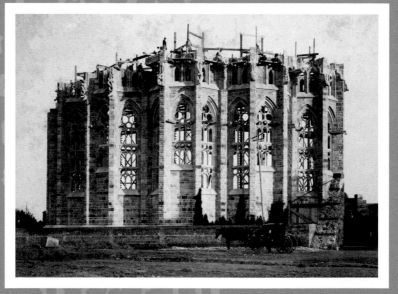

THE APSE -IN A PHOTOGRAPH TAKEN AROUND 1892- WAS BUILT IMMEDIATELY
AFTER THE CRYPT AND POSSESSES THE SAME ARCHITECTURAL STYLE

←
AERIAL VIEW FROM OF THE APSE (2004)

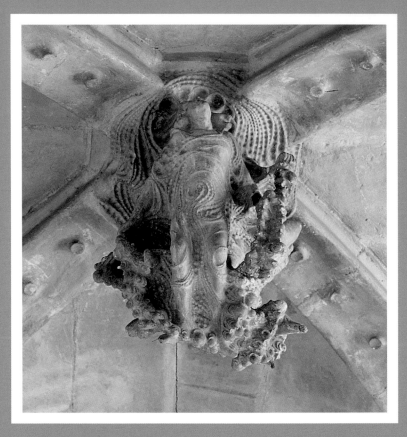

ANGEL IN THE KEYSTONE OF THE CHAPEL OF THE ROSARY

The Apse and the Cloister

During the first years of construction, Gaudí was little interested in religion and much more interested in social life. A dandy in his dress, wearing elegant well-cut clothes, top hat and black gloves, he generally went to the building site in a horse and carriage. Once there, he stayed seated inside while the plans were brought to him so that he could give orders to his foremen, remembers César Martinell.

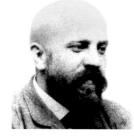

GAUDÍ IN 1888

Once the crypt had been finished, he had the apse built above it, with a further seven chapels and two stairs on the two sides that continue the spiral staircases from the crypt. Inside the apse there are two good-sized stone snails, indicating the presence of the staircases.

At a future date, a soaring dome will be built over the apse, dedicated to the Virgin, so that crypt, apse and dome will form a single whole devoted to the worship of Our Lady, as well as containing a door from the cloister opening onto the street, dedicated to the Assumption.

Worship of Mary, which had grown up in within the Christian church based on a few scant references in the gospels, underwent tremendous expansion after the Council of Trent and was at its zenith in the nineteenth century. Gaudí was not the least of the artists of the time to extol the Virgin.

Also in Gothic style, the apse was completed in 1893. With its walls, windows and pinnacles, it shows a greater inventiveness on Gaudí's part, so that he was able to say, "this architecture is a perfecting of the Gothic style". Just a few years later he could have said that he had gone beyond it completely.

The interior of the apse is decorated with heads of angels and clusters of tears reminding us of suffering. On the outside, the parts illuminated by the sun contrast with those in the shade. Frogs, dragons, lizards, snakes and salamanders cling to the outside of the building, "without being able to come in", because of their moderately demoniacal nature, yet doing the beneficial work of gargoyles in channelling off the rainwater. The pinnacles atop the walls are grasses, including ears of wheat, representing the sublime heights of religion.

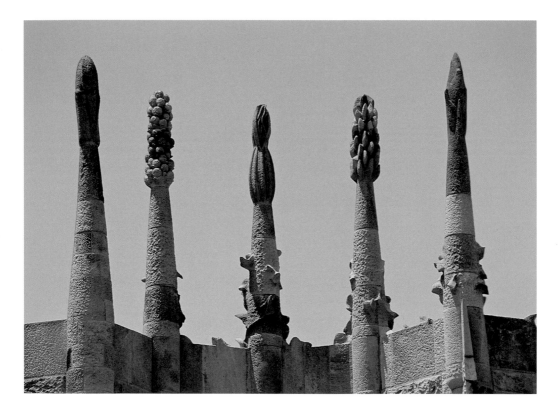

PINNACLES INSPIRED BY BOTANICAL FORMS THAT CROWN THE APSE WALLS

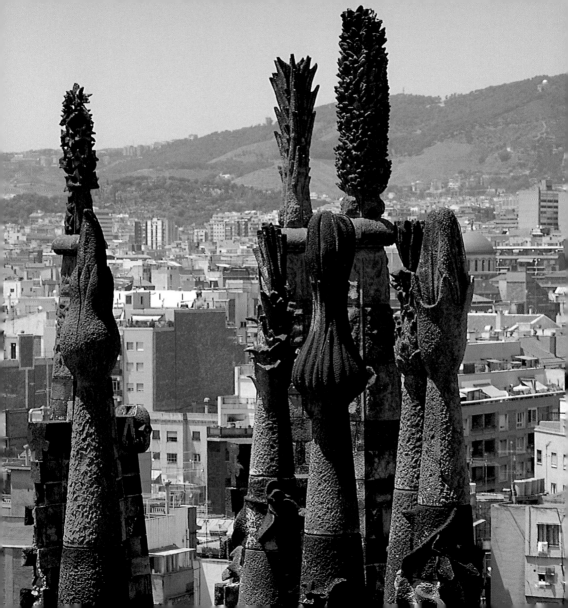

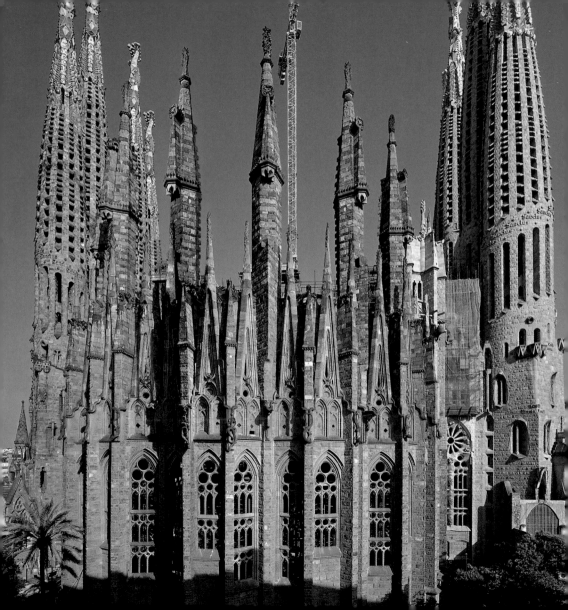

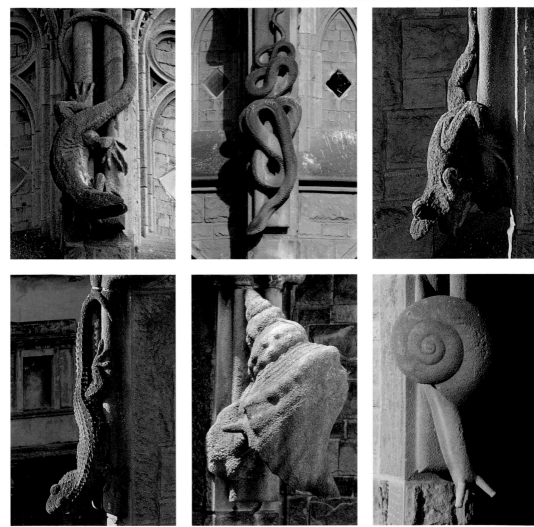

THE GARGOYLES REPRESENT MOLLUSCS, AMPHIBIANS AND REPTILES

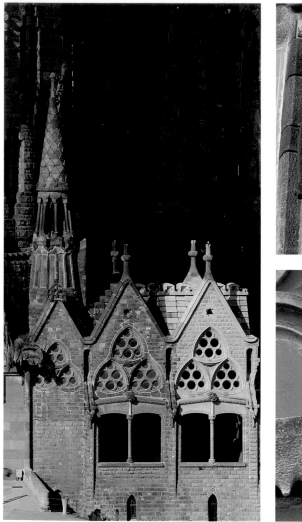

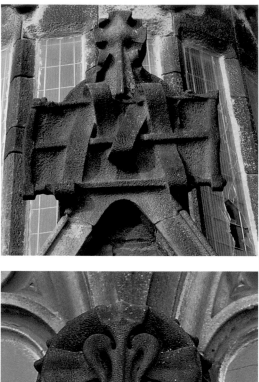

EXTERIOR OF THE CHAPEL OF THE ROSARY. THE SHAVINGS FORM THE 'M' INTERWOVEN WITH THE CARPENTER'S SAW AND ANAGRAM OF MARY

Cloister

Although it is thought of as a church, the Sagrada Familia is a site enclosing numerous buildings, besides the church building itself. The site takes up almost all the block, with the four sides forming the cloister, the latter only partly built as yet. This might seem strange, since in monasteries and cathedrals, cloisters are the interior channels that give access to the different areas. Gaudí, on the other hand, gives the cloister the exact function that its Latin name suggests: *claudere*, to enclose. And indeed, here the cloister encloses the gigantic church and the rest of the architecture –the baptistry, the sacristies and other chapels and other buildings– on the outside, not on the inside. In this aspect too, Gaudí is the innovator and perfectionist of European religious tradition.

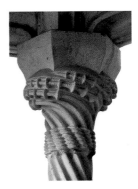

CAPITAL IN THE CLOISTER

The cloister acts, as the architect himself has said, to gather in oneself, to say a prayer while walking, or hold processions when the weather is bad, and most importantly of all, keep the street noise from penetrating as far as is possible. It is also the modern reflex of the wall that protected the monasteries in the Middle Ages.

The four sides of the rectangle are the four façades or "fronts" of the Sagrada Familia, whose entrances interrupt the continuity of the cloister, though not completely, since they do not bar your way. These are the Nativity and Passion entrances, at either end of the transept, and the Glory entrance at the end of the nave, with the discrete Assumption Door at the opposite end, with side entrances into the Crypt.

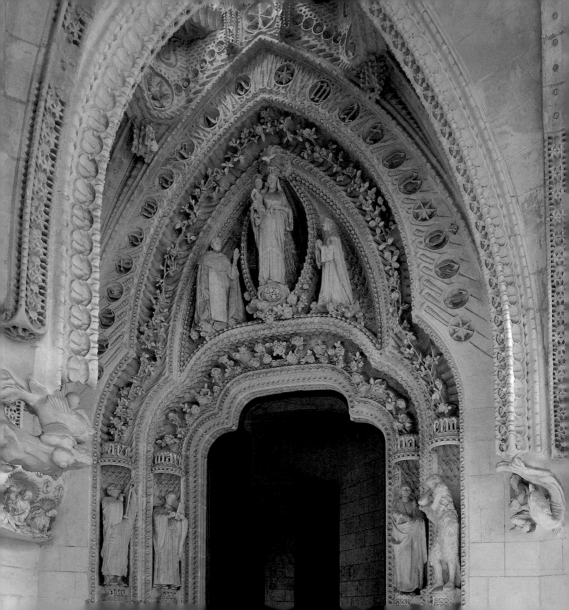

Chapel of the Rosary

Of the two chapels situated at the corners of the cloister, Gaudí was only responsible for the chapel of Our Lady of the Rosary. This is quite a small construction, but it has a domed ceiling that fills it with light and which is extraordinarily decorated as if the walls were made of lace, with a great profusion of roses, rose bushes and rosaries, since all of these are Christian symbols. Among the figures to be found in this chapel, besides the Virgin and Child, are certain saints, including Saint Dominic and Saint Catherine of Sienna, and on each side of the door are kings and prophets of the Old Testament such as David, Solomon, Isaac and Jacob.

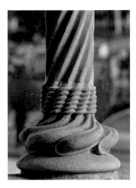

BASE OF A MULLION IN
THE CHAPEL OF THE ROSARY

Particularly striking is the representation of the death of the just man, with the text: "And in the hour of our death, Amen", written in Latin –in which the Virgin presents the child to a dying man, while Saint Joseph accompanies him in his last moments.

The groups most remarked upon by visitors to the Sagrada Familia are the Temptations. The first shows a woman being given a bag of money by a diabolical monster in the shape of a fish, resembling a hogfish. The second shows a man tempted by another devil, this time in the form of an eel with an Orsini hand bomb, the sort most favoured at that time by direct action anarchists. But both the woman and the man overcome the temptation by dedicating themselves to the Virgin, who looks at them lovingly.

In the dome, there are three etherial angel figures who dance and play joyfully with foam taken from the waters, a prodigious image of turning stone into froth.

DOORWAY OF THE CHAPEL OF THE ROSARY IN THE CLOISTER

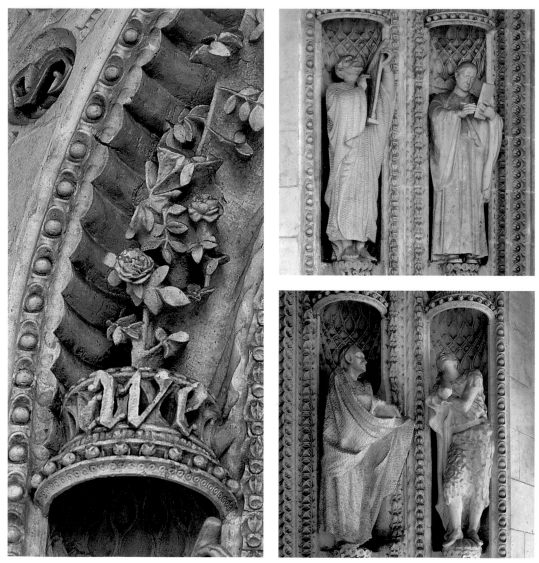

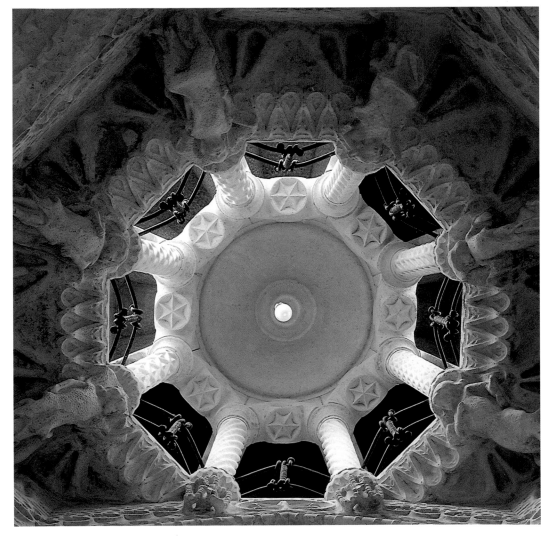

CUPOLA LETTING IN THE LIGHT TO THE CHAPEL OF THE ROSARY
← ROSES REFERRING TO THE DEDICATION TO THE VIRGIN | DAVID AND SOLOMON | ISAAC AND JACOB

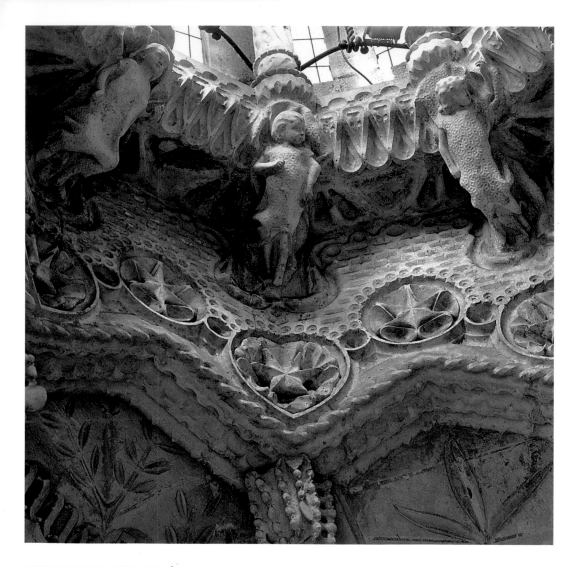

ANGELS ON THE CUPOLA OF THE CHAPEL | DETAIL OF THE ELABORATE ORNAMENTATION COVERING THE WALLS

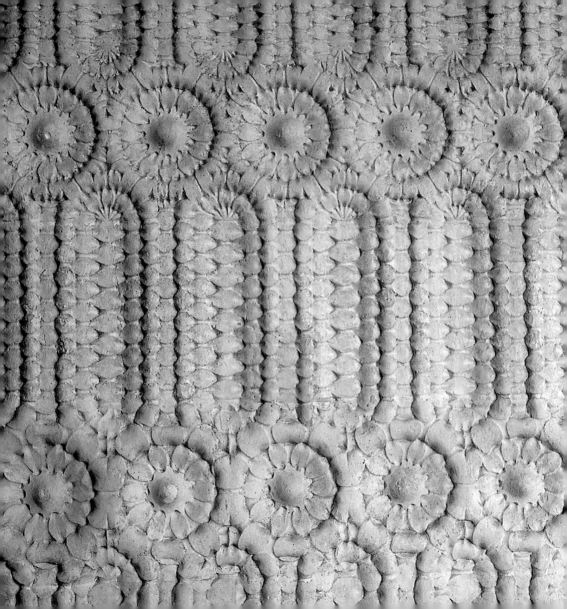

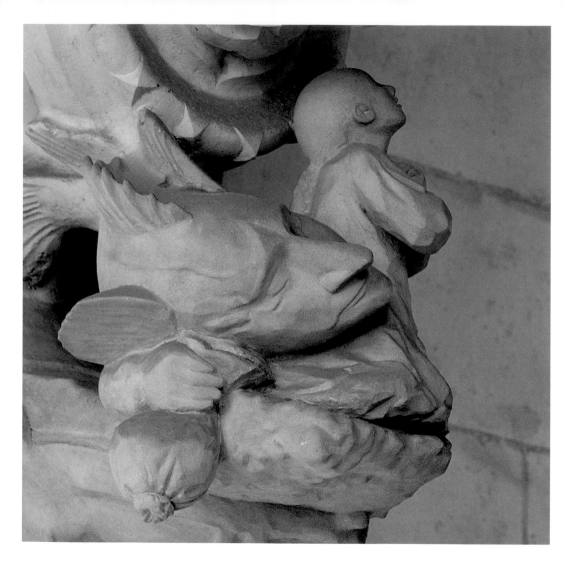

VANITY, THE TEMPTATION OF WOMAN: A DEMON OFFERS A BAG OF MONEY

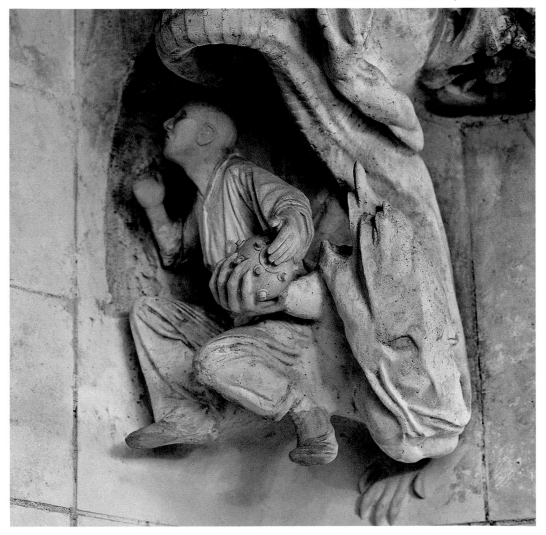

VIOLENCE, THE TEMPTATION OF MAN: A DIABOLICAL FIGURE PLACES AN ORSINI BOMB (THE TYPE
USED IN THE BOMBING OF THE LICEO THEATRE IN BARCELONA) IN THE HANDS OF A WORKER

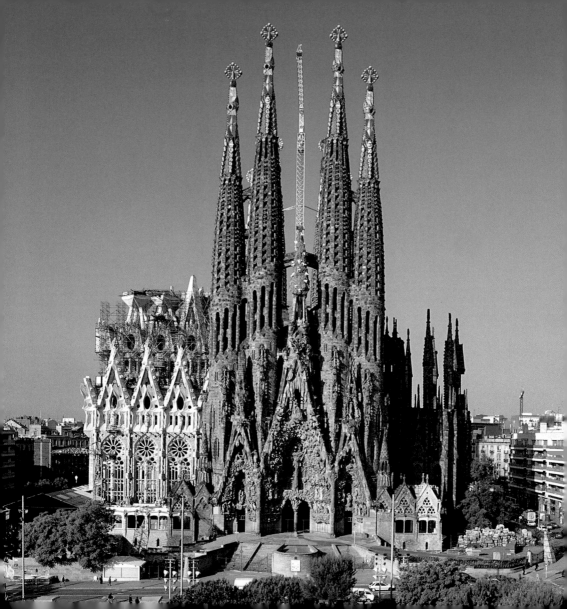

The Nativity Façade

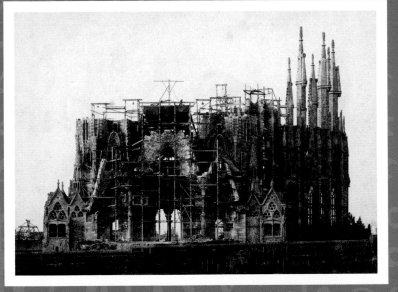

POSITIONING TESTS OF THE PLASTER MODEL FOR THE CHARITY DOORWAY ARCHIVOLT IN FEBRUARY 1898. IN THE SIDE DOORWAYS THE PARABOLIC ARCHES USED FOR THE FIRST TIME IN THE TEMPLE IN 1897 CAN BE SEEN

←
THE NATIVITY FAÇADE

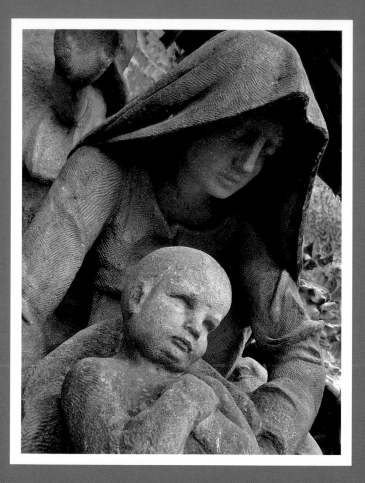

VIRGIN AND CHILD, CENTRAL MOTIF OF THE NATIVITY FAÇADE

The Nativity Façade

Antoni Gaudí once said: "...in the Sagrada Familia all is providential. From the very beginning, when we started the façade which we are just now finishing, a lady made a donation of 140,000 *duros* (700,000 pesetas) making it possible to carry out the project on a considerably more lavish scale than the modest one we had originally envisaged. The work was then able to take on the magnificence which it would not have had, thanks to the generosity of the then administrator who asked me to spend as much as possible on the building, fearing that Dr. Català, appointed Bishop of Barcelona in 1883, would spend the money elsewhere." (according to C. Martinell).

On another occasion, Gaudí was more specific: "First we were given 60,000 *duros*, and then a further 70,000 *duros*; that is why we built the Nativity entrance and the plaster model of the archivolt, which cost 20,000 *duros*. Twelve carpenters were working on it for a year, making the moulds" (according to Puig i Boada). All we know of the donor is that her name was Isabel.

There were frequent tensions between orders or groups –for example between the Josephine order and the Bishop– because their respective interests did not coincide. At all events, these facts gleaned from Gaudí help to explain the economic foundation to the grandiose and exuberant concept that was the Sagrada Familia.

The Nativity Façade was the first to be completed, and the building work took the last two decades of the 19th century and the first third of the 20th. There are three great doors, the central one higher than those on either side, and four belfries. These break away, to an extent, from the Gothic

ANTONI GAUDÍ IN 1920

→
THE NATIVITY FAÇADE FEATURES
TWO SALOMONIC COLUMNS
WITH PALM TREE CAPITALS
THAT DIVIDE THE THREE
DOORWAYS. OVER THEM ARE
THE TRUMPETING ANGELS

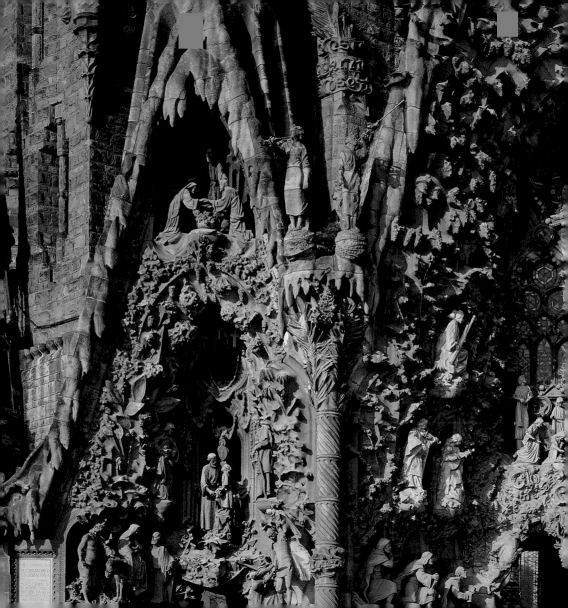

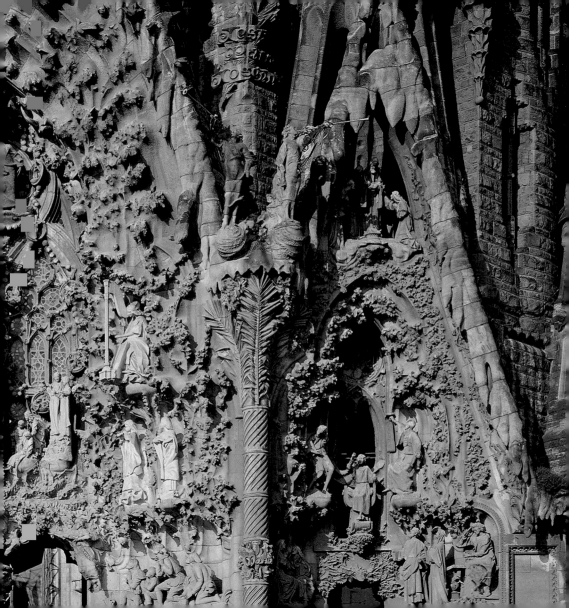

style, especially in the case of the belfries which are stunningly original. The three porticos are dedicated to the principal dogmas of the Catholic church, as well as to Jesus' origins, childhood and adolescence, according to the Gospels.

The triple façade forms a unified landscape, against which the human figure stands out. It is the wonder of nature in nascent state, creator of all that exists and in constant transformation.

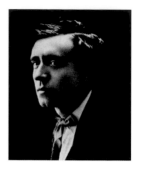

If we gaze now at the finished Nativity Façade, we can see two tall, elaborate columns between the three doorways. Each of these is mounted on a tortoise, the one nearest the sea is a sea tortoise (or turtle) and the one on the inland side is a land tortoise. Tortoises symbolise the unchanging and, in traditional Chinese culture much studied in the West at the end of the 19th century, they guarantee the stability of the cosmos. At the same time, the great chameleons that go from one side of the façade to the other surely represent constant change in the natural world.

What is more, Gaudí originally wanted this façade to be multicoloured, something that the spectator has difficulty even imagining. "The lower part of the façades (...) where there are scenes full of human figures and natural things, will be painted". He also says," The coloured model that is in the church workshops displays the tones that will be used in the Nativity doors: midnight blue in the middle for Christmas; light green for the Egyptian scenes, recalling the Nile; sienna for the door on the right, setting the scene in Palestine" (according to Puig i Boada).

Gaudí thought that this exterior paintwork would not be spoilt by the weather since it was protected from the sun and rain, while "the rest, open to the kiss of the sun, the great painter of our land, will gradually go golden and red by itself", to use his own words.

Also, between the Hope door and that of Christian Love and between the latter and the Faith door, there are four angels with trumpets, who are not announcing the Good News but rather the end of the world. These four figures are full of life, and perhaps the most interesting to be sculpted for the cathedral.

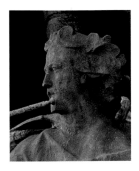

ANGEL FOR WHICH OPISSO
POSED AS A MODEL

According to draughtsman Ricardo Opisso, Gaudí was talking one day with Torres i Bages, formerly Bishop of Vic, when a band of trumpeters began to create such a racket that Gaudí was outraged and stalked towards them with the intention of shutting them up. But when he was about to give vent to his ire as on other occasions, he caught sight of the officer in charge, who turned out to be the son of a close friend of Gaudí's. He took his music elsewhere.

The architect used three of the trumpet players as models for the angels, while he used Opisso himself for the fourth. Opisso was very young in those days and at times infuriated him with his unruly behaviour. It was typical of Gaudí paradoxically to immortalise him in this way.

Opisso recalled years after, the day that Gaudí found out he had been to a café-concert, and summoned him with a shattering "Master Opisso, come here!" and ordered him to kneel with an even more ingenuous if irritated "Chastise yourself, sir."

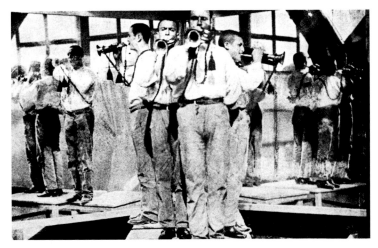

GAUDÍ PLANNED THE SCULPTURES FOR
THE FAÇADE IN GREAT DETAIL. WITH
AN INGENIOUS SYSTEM OF MIRRORS HE
WAS ABLE TO OBTAIN SEVERAL POINTS
OF VIEW OF THE MODEL IN JUST ONE
PHOTOGRAPH

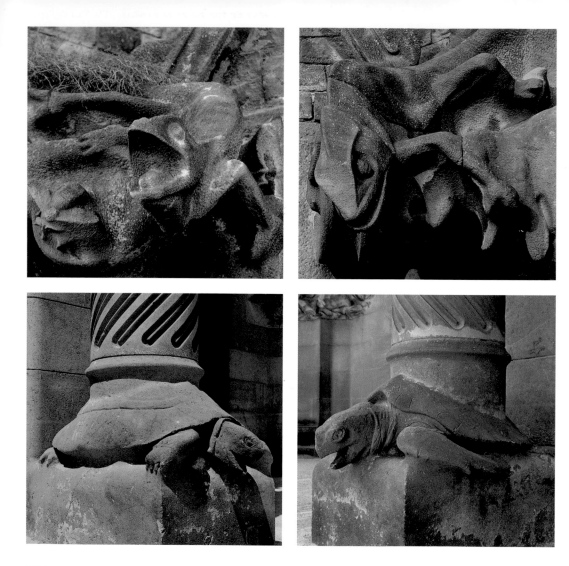

THE CHAMELEONS, ON THE LEFT AND RIGHT OF THE FAÇADE, AND THE TORTOISES AND TURTLES, WHICH "SUPPORT" THE COLUMNS

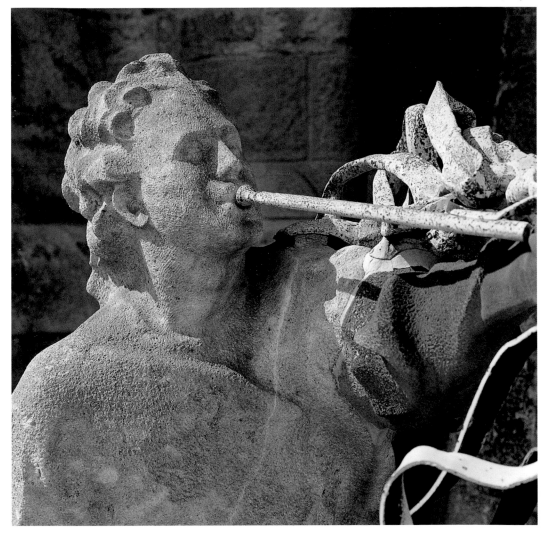

THE TRUMPETING ANGELS CRY OUT TO THE FOUR WINDS OF THE EARTH

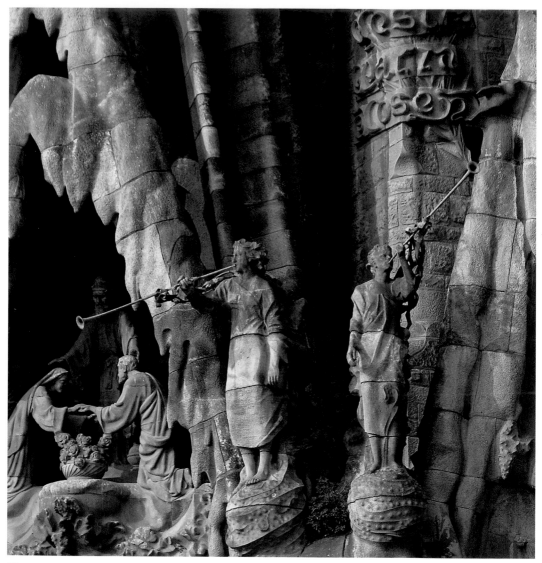

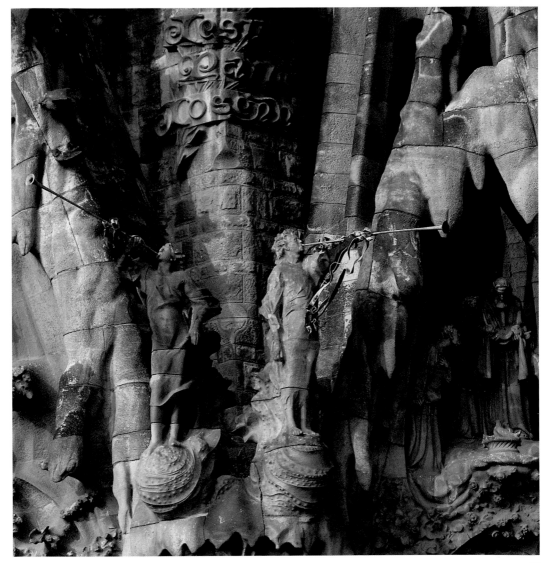

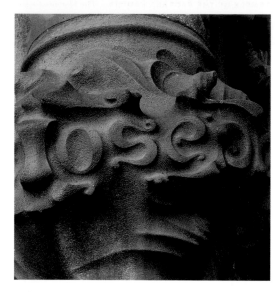

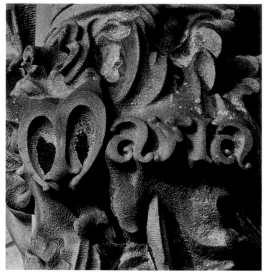

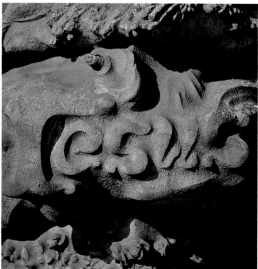

INSCRIPTIONS IN RELIEF OF THE NAMES OF THE SAGRADA
FAMILIA (HOLY FAMILY) ON THE SALOMONIC COLUMNS

—

THE NAME OF JESUS APPEARS ON THE MULLION OF THE MAIN
DOORWAY, AND THOSE OF MARY AND JOSEPH ON THE SIDE COLUMNS

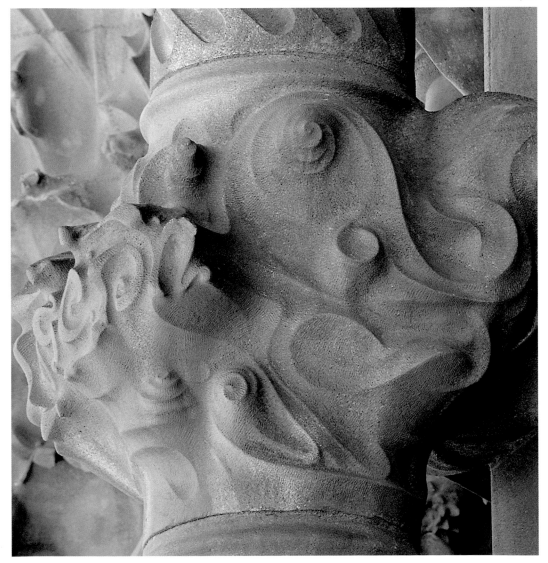

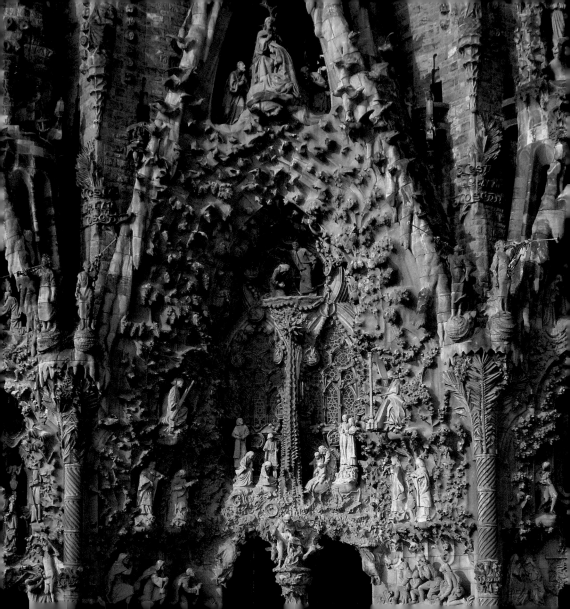

Charity Doorway

The middle doorway, named for Charity or Christian Love, "expresses the verve and joy of life" according to Gaudí, and is both the entrance to the cathedral and porch of Bethlehem in the form of the cave.

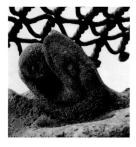

ON THE MULLION BASE THE SNAKE WITH THE FORBIDDEN FRUIT

The doorway is divided in two by a column, and wound around the latter from top to bottom is the serpent with the apple of sin in its mouth. The reason why Jesus came into the world to save it, and from top to bottom, a ribbon with the names of all Jesus' forebears since Abraham.

Above is the Nativity: Joseph protects Mary and both of them adore Jesus, with the ox and the ass of popular tradition on either side. Around them are cherubs who gaze joyfully at the newborn babe. The star, whose comet tail emerges from the Nativity scene, shines on high with all the strength of Gaudí's art. And, guided by it, the shepherds and Magi go towards the doorway. On the next levels, emulating many medieval cathedrals, musician angels, male and female, six in number, play learned instruments (harp, bassoon and viola) and popular ones (zither, drum and *dulzaina*, a type of clainet) as befitted an era, the *Renaixença* or Catalan 19th century Renaissance, which looked with equal admiration at the learned and the popular.

To produce the many sculptures that must illustrate and adorn the church both outside and inside, Gaudí employed the method of making casts of the faces of the people working on the cathedral, and of the children, women and men who died in the Hospital de la Santa Cruz. Later, he took several photographs of each from different angles, using mirrors. Gaudí and his assistants had a well-equipped photographic studio from which we have many photographs. What was perhaps innovative about Gaudí's approach was calculating the degree of distortion involved with each figure, depending on the greater or lesser height from the ground that each was situated, so that they would all appear of natural size when seen from below.

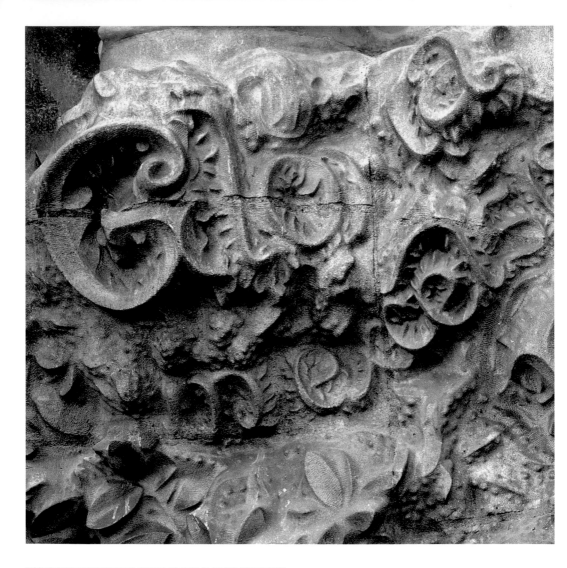

INSCRIPTION READING "GLORIA IN EXCELSIS DEO", GLORY TO GOD ON HIGH

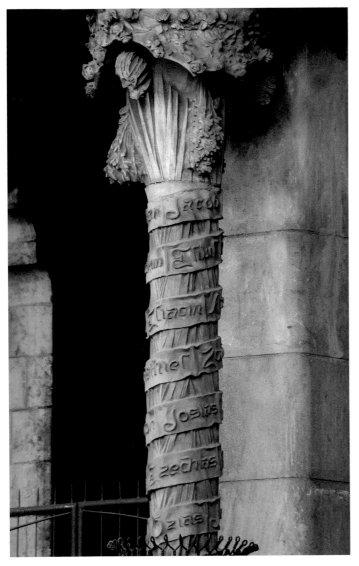

THE NATIVITY SCENE IS SUPPORTED BY A PALM TREE-COLUMN WITH THE PALM FRONDS GATHERED BY A HELICOIDAL STRIP WITH THE GENEALOGY OF JESUS CHRIST. THE COLUMN IS ENVELOPED BY A WROUGHT-IRON GRILLE, THE RESULT OF THE INTERWEAVING OF A SINGLE THREAD OF IRON

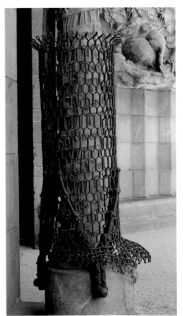

THE NATIVITY SURROUNDED BY
SIX MUSICIAN ANGELS –PLAYING
THE HARP, BASSOON, ZITHER,
VIOLA, DRUM AND "DULZAINA",
A TYPE OF CLARINET– AND
A CHOIR OF CHILD ANGELS.
THE SCULPTURES OF THE
ANGELS HAVE BEEN PRODUCED
RECENTLY BY THE JAPANESE
SCULPTOR ETSURO SOTOO

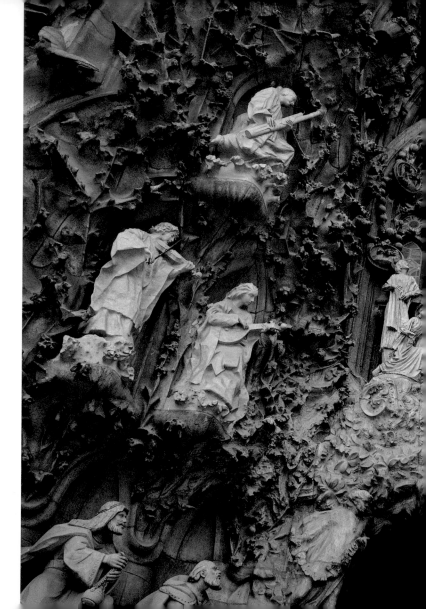

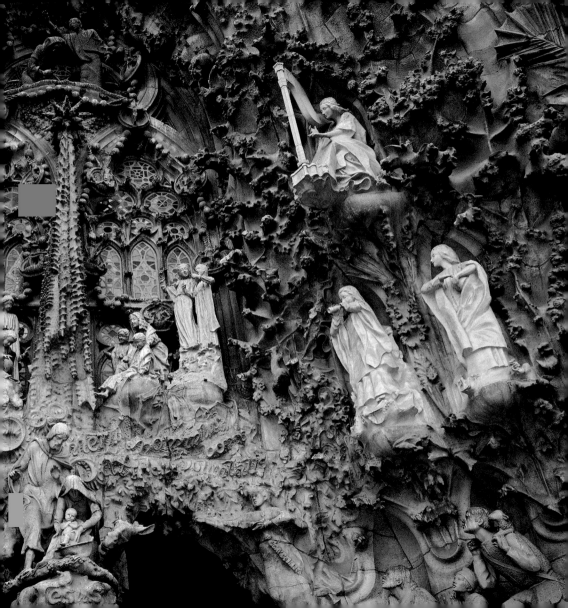

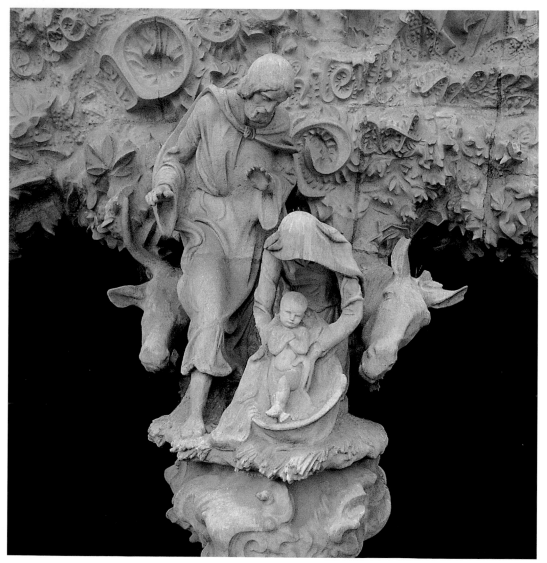

A number of different artists made the figures on the Nativity Façade, above all Juan Matamala, under Gaudí's direction, who indicated that he wanted figures or groups to occupy the different areas of the façade and indeed the whole of the church. After his death, some assistant sculptors worked to the plans, photographs and notes of the master, where these existed, and invented them when necessary. Among these, Busquets and Sotoo have to be mentioned, as well as Subirachs.

Of greater aesthetic interest, in the lower area of the portal, are the very elaborate inscriptions carried by the angels, where we read in Latin, "Jesus has been born. Come and adore him" and, next to the doors, "Glory to God on the high and peace on Earthand goodwill to men

On the next level there is a rose window decorated with a rosary, and superimposed on this, the sculptural group of the Incarnation. This work by Joan Tusquets, following Gaudí's plans, depicts the angel placing his hand on Mary. The Incarnation is earlier in time than the Nativity, showing that Gaudí is not presenting things in chronological order so much as thematically. In this door the theme is Love, and as an instance of divine love, the Incarnation is shown. Strange to say, all this is surrounded by a great work in relief, representing the first half of the zodiac to indicate the time the birth took place.

Despite their size, it is not easy at first sight to distinguish the figures that make up this zodiac design –you need to look very carefully. Going from left to right in a large arc you have: Aries the ram, Taurus with his great horns, Gemini the twins, and almost in the centre, Cancer the crab, then the lion of Leo, and lastly the young woman of Virgo. The zodiac is a pagan representation of human destiny marked out by the stars and, as such, repeatedly forbidden by the church which teaches that man is free. Nonetheless, since the time of the Crusades, astrology has occupied an important place in both lay and religious culture, and there have been many Christian astrologers and innumerable references to astrology in churches and cathedrals. Gaudí, then, gave them a place in his cathedral.

In the upper cave, formed by icicles, Mary is crowned Queen of Heaven by Jesus. The work was executed by Matamala, as planned by Gaudí. It is a clear sign of the great veneration that the Catholic church has accorded the Virgin almost since its beginnings, a veneration that reached its peak in the second half of the 19th century. This representation is different from usual, since Jesus places the crown, while Saint Joseph presides, staff

ON SAINT JOSEPH'S DAY 1958, THE NATIVITY GROUP PRODUCED BY J. BUSQUETS WAS PLACED OVER THE GENEALOGICAL COLUMN

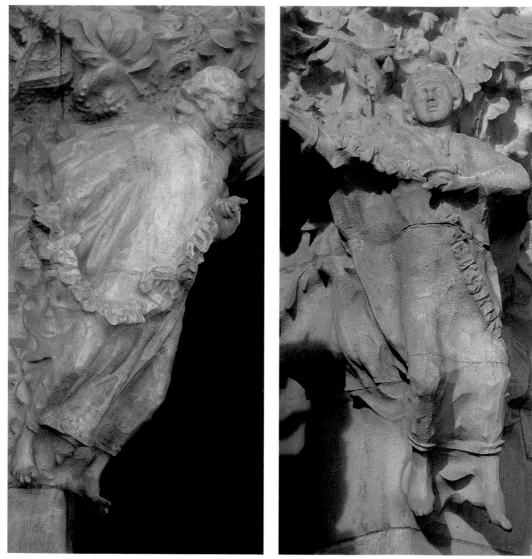

in hand, replacing God the Father –this, to give Joseph the central role in a church consecrated to him. The Holy Spirit is replaced by a third man, half-concealed in the mid ground, worshipping Mary. Perhaps he is a blessed representative of the Josephine Order.

A drawing of falling bodies, done in 1900 by the young Opisso at Gaudí's behest, was used as the model for the eye-catching angels on the reverse side of the Coronation window. The latter fall in mid-flight, while singing the Sanctus Deus. They have their mouths open, but appear to be unseeing –in fact, despite the resounding inscriptions of their songs, they seem to be lifeless bodies. Most probably they were originally meant to be painted, which would completely alter their somewhat unsettling expression.

THE ANGELS POSITIONED BELOW THE NATIVITY SCENE ARE CARRYING SASHES THAT READ, "JESUS HAS BEEN BORN. COME AND ADORE HIM", AND, "GLORY TO GOD ON HIGH AND PEACE ON EARTH AND GOODWILL TO MEN"

—

ETSURO SOTOO (FUKUOKA, JAPAN, 1953) HAS WORKED ON THE SAGRADA FAMILIA SINCE 1978. THE SCULPTOR IS A FERVENT ADMIRER OF GAUDÍ AND, LIKE THE ARCHITECT, LOOKS FOR THE SOURCES OF HIS INSPIRATION IN NATURE AND CATHOLICISM. AMONG THE SCULPTURES HE HAS CREATED FOR THE TEMPLE FEATURE THE CELESTIAL CHOIR AND THE MUSICIAN ANGELS THAT ARE PLACED AROUND THE NATIVITY SCENE

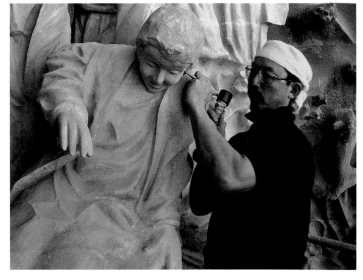

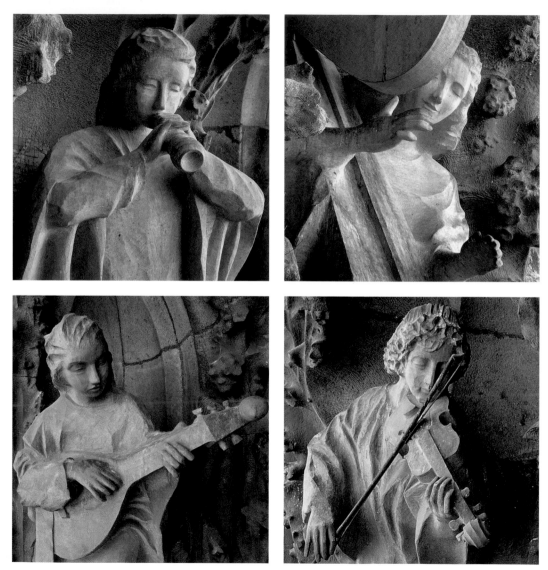

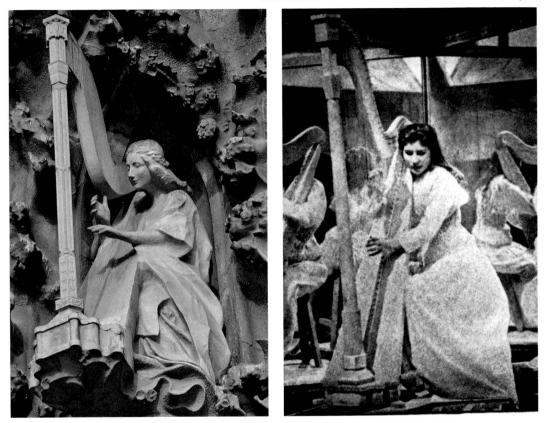

GAUDÍ USED THE LOCAL PEOPLE TO CREATE THE CHARACTERS FOR THE ORNAMENTATION OF THE SAGRADA FAMILIA. THE TEMPLE WORKERS, THEIR FAMILIES, THE CHILDREN FROM THE PARISH SCHOOL AND NEIGHBOURS ALL CAME TO THE TEMPLE TO HAVE THEIR PORTRAITS TAKEN AND TO POSE AS MODELS. THE ARCHITECT, ACCORDING TO HIS BIOGRAPHER, J. RÀFOLS, "WANTED TO REPRODUCE LIFE JUST AS IT IS, AS IF LIFE AND ART WERE THE SAME THING...". DESPITE THE DESTRUCTION OF THE PLASTER MODELS OF THE MUSICIAN ANGELS DURING THE SPANISH CIVIL WAR, SOME OF THOSE OLD PHOTOGRAPHS HAVE ENABLED E. SOTOO TO BE ABLE TO FAITHFULLY FOLLOW THE GUIDELINES SET OUT BY GAUDÍ

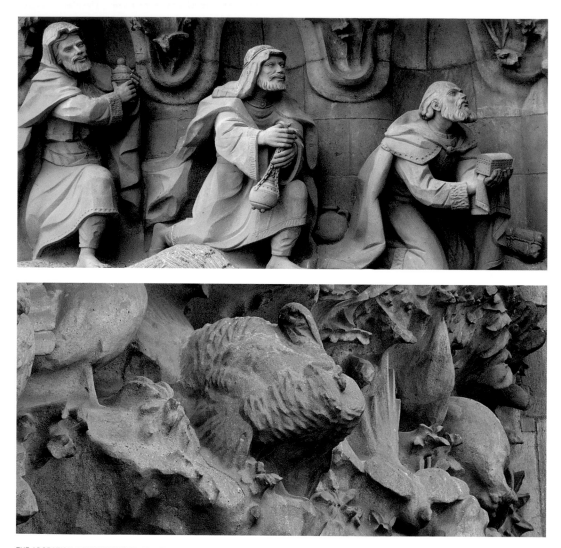

THE ADORATION OF THE THREE KINGS APPEARS LIKE A MONUMENTAL NATIVITY SCENE AND, ON THEIR PEDESTAL,
CHICKENS FROM THE CHRISTMAS FEAST

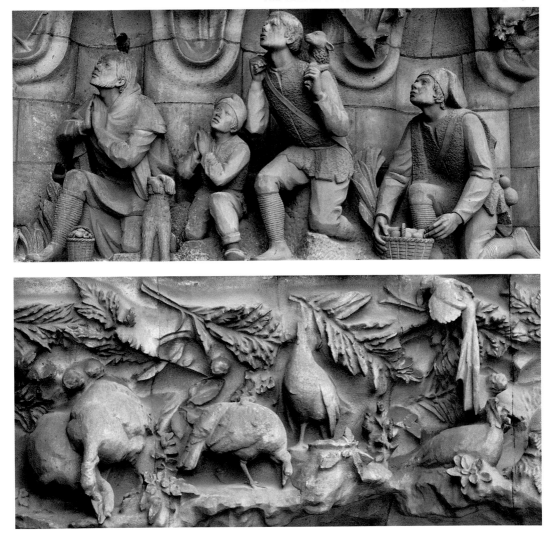

THE ADORATION OF THE SHEPHERDS AND ITS CORRESPONDING BASE FULL OF ANIMAL AND PLANT MOTIFS

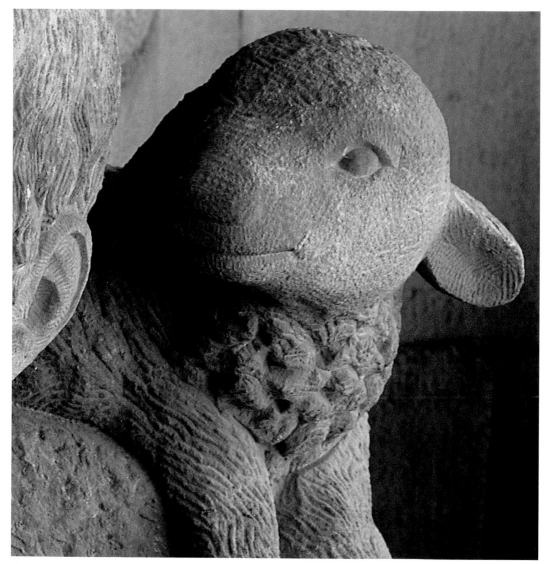

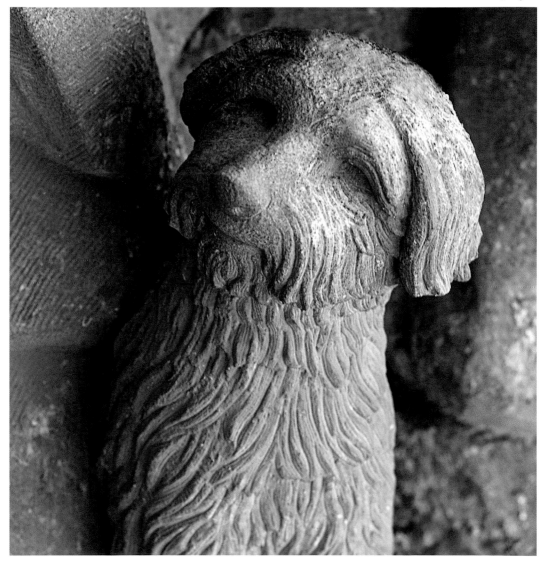

LIKE A HYMN TO LIFE, AN INFINITE
NUMBER OF ANIMALS AND
PLANTS EMERGE WITH VIGOUR
FROM THE INERT STONE. THE
FERTILITY OF NATURE HERALDS
THE BIRTH OF THE SAVIOUR AND
CELEBRATES THE ARRIVAL OF A
NEW AND REGENERATED WORLD

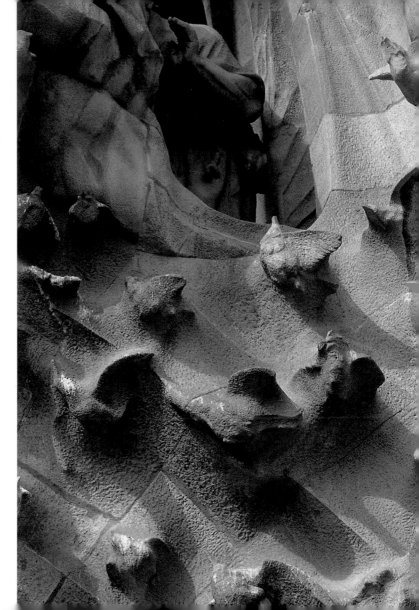

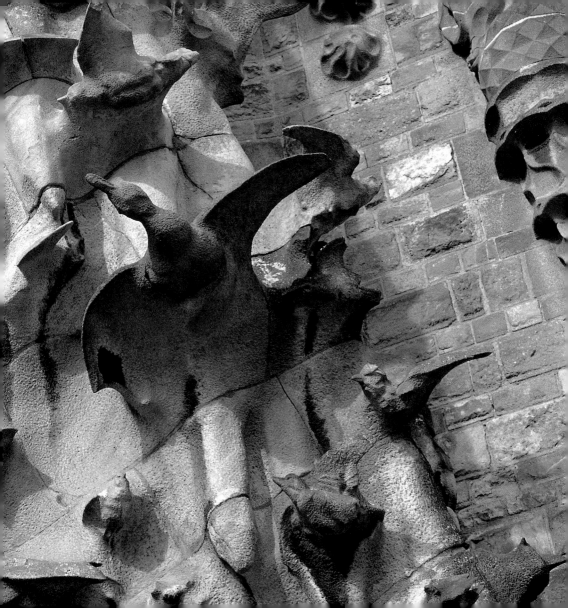

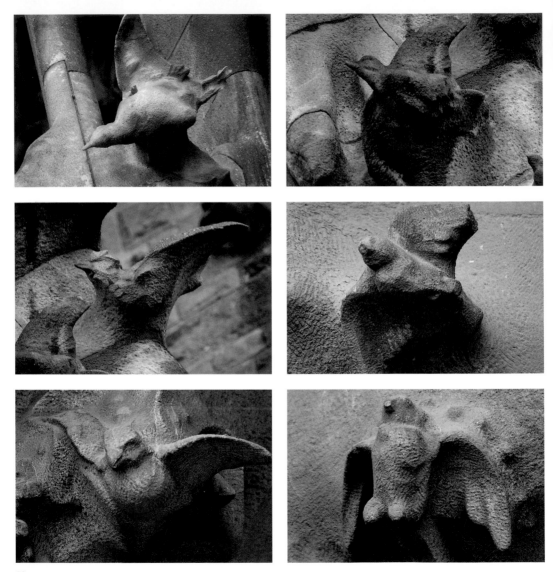

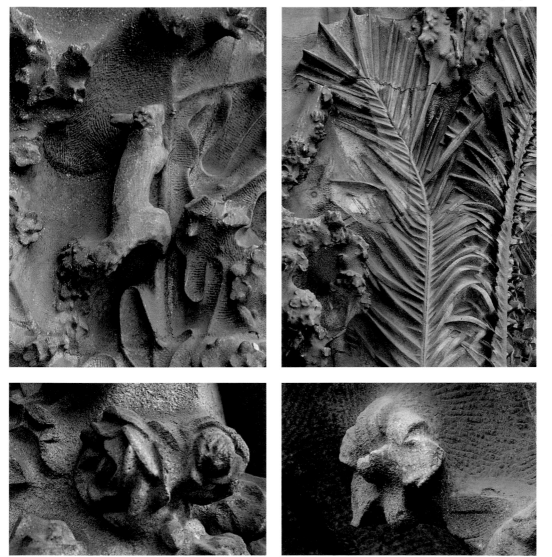

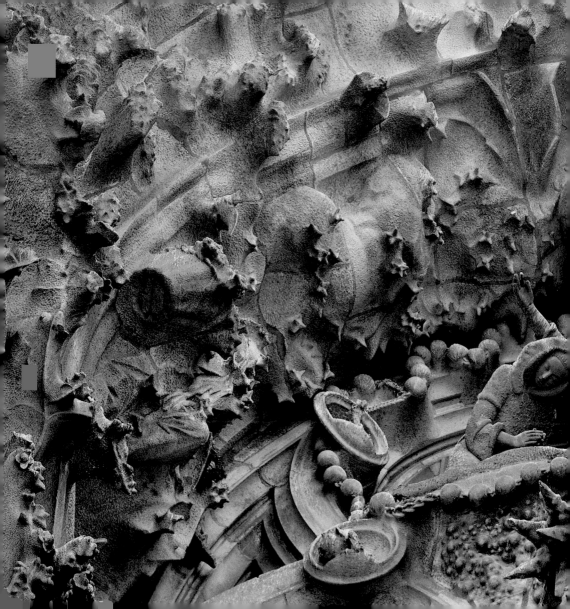

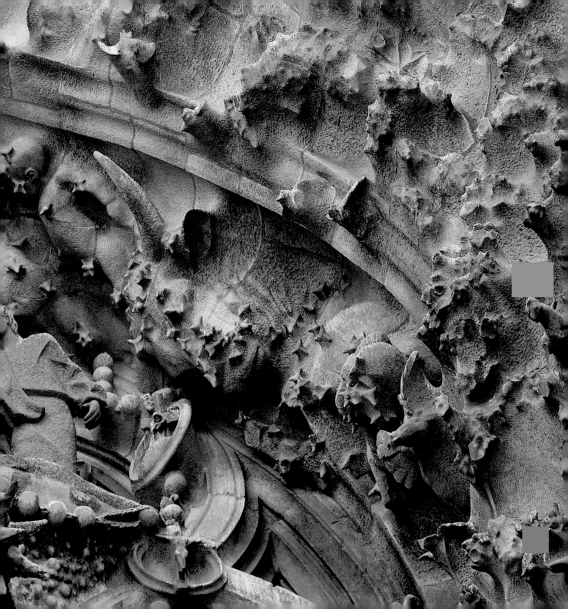

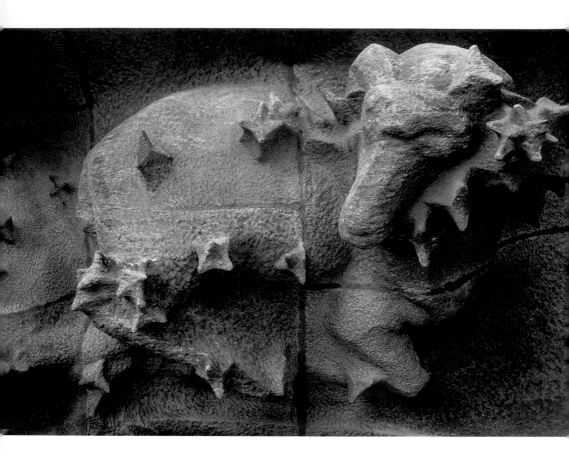

REPRESENTATION OF THE CONSTELLATION OF ARIES
←
THE STARRY NIGHT FRAMES THE INCARNATION OF THE WORD ON THE NATIVITY DOORWAY

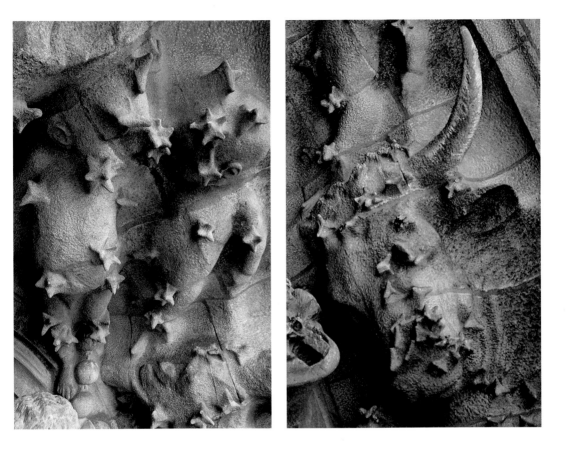

GEMINI AND TAURUS

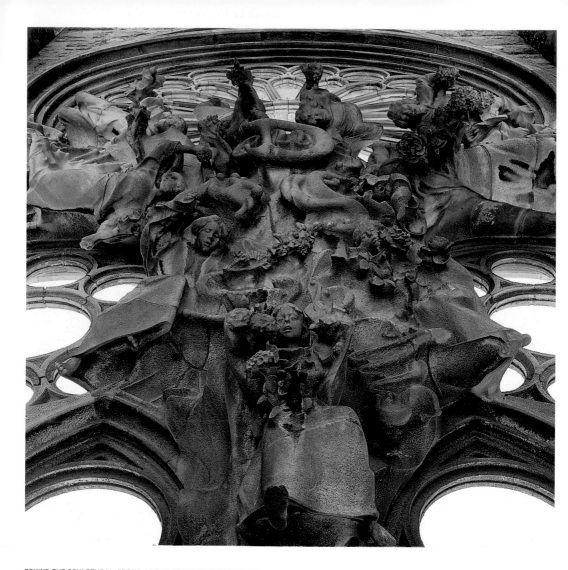

BEHIND THE SCULPTURAL GROUP OF THE CORONATION OF THE VIRGIN, WE COME ACROSS A ROSE WINDOW WITH ANGELS SINGING THE SANCTUS DEUS

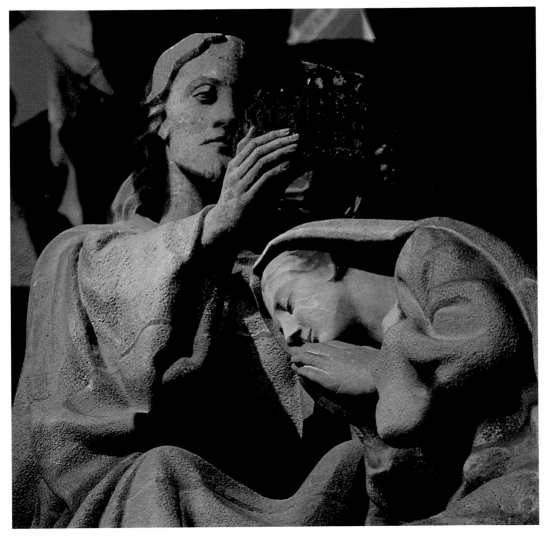

CORONATION OF MARY

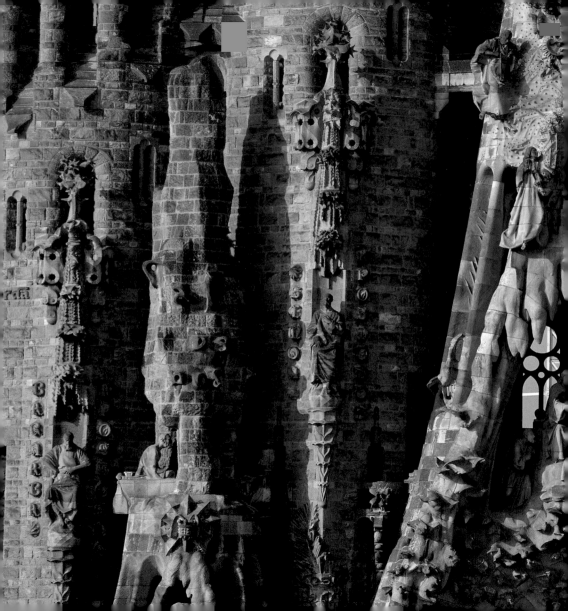

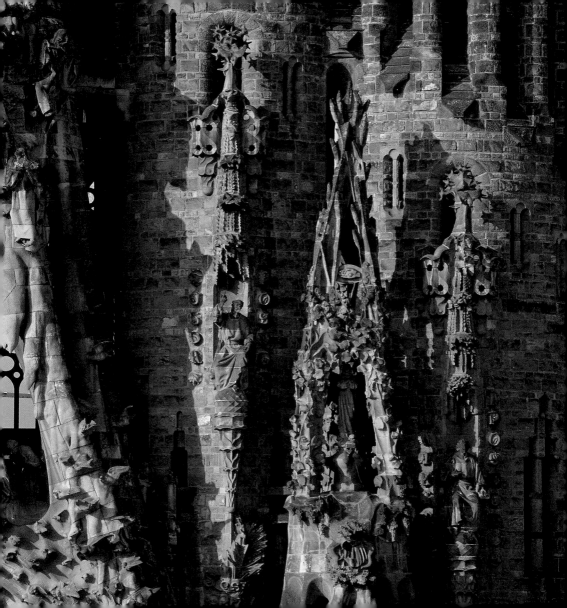

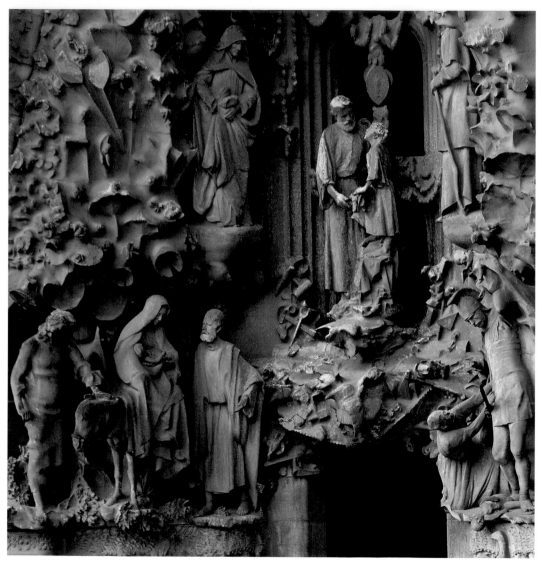

Hope Doorway

To the left of the central portal is the Hope Door, dedicated to this theological virtue, although the examples that Gaudí gives in the shape of the sculptural groups are not exactly hope-inspiring, quite the contrary. But this should be interpreted as the hope sustained by the believer even in the face of adversity.

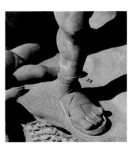

SIX-TOED FOOT OF
THE ROMAN SOLDIER

Following the Nativity, according to the Gospels, came the Slaughter of the Innocents on Herod's orders. The executioner who is about to put the child to the sword with the horrified mother begging him to stop, is actually modelled on a giant of chap. When they came to make a mould of him, they found he had six toes on each foot. The sculptor, Matamala, wanted to cover up the defect, but Gaudí forbad him to do so on the principle that the monstrous nature of the killing should be reflected in the monstrosity of the feet (according to Descharnes). The stage known as the Flight into Egypt can be seen on the same level, represented by a shining angel who guides the ass carrying the Virgin and Child, while Joseph looks anxiously on.

On the upper level there is a child, almost certainly Jesus, carrying a wounded or dead dove to show to a wise man (Joseph, or an old priest). Saint Ann and Saint Joachim, Jesus' maternal grandparents, watch them. Perhaps all this is based on the Gospel according to Saint Luke (2, 22-24), where it says that they went up to the temple with Jesus to present him to the Lord and offer up a pair of turtle doves as a sacrifice. There are other interpretations, however. Before continuing it would be worthwhile observing the arch over the door, below these groups. It takes the form of a great woodman's saw, with handles at either end. Above the saw are a large number of tools, belonging to different crafts, all related to building. The Gospels never say that Joseph was a carpenter, they use the term *technos*, that is to say a craftsman, without specifying the craft. The *technos* were those who traditionally built the houses, whether of stone or wood, or indeed both. This must have appealed to Gaudí, and thus on the floor there are such diverse implements

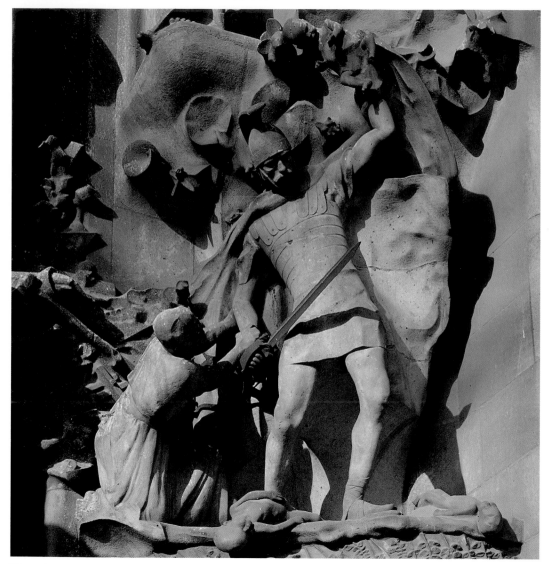

as a hammer, an axe, a carpenter's square, a mallet, a screw-driver, etc, all of them builders' tools. Around the window there is a rosary, as befits an era when praying the rosary as a family became very popular in Spain, especially Catalonia. Above this is the betrothal of Mary and Joseph.

Saint Joseph appears on the next level, seated in a boat, and before him is a very large lamp and a canopy with the Holy Spirit hovering above it. The boat, with the anchor ready to cast, is seeking refuge in a cave. Many observers have seen the lamp as lighting the way for the church in the night of ages, and Saint Joseph's guiding of the boat as a celebration of having been chosen by the Catholic Church as its patron.

Topping off this portal is a great crag, which many have taken to be Montserrat, Catalonia's sacred mountain: on the side of the peak is the legend, *Sal-va-nos* (Save us).

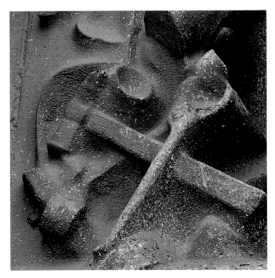

THE SLAUGHTER OF THE INNOCENTS

—

BUILDER AND CARPENTER'S TOOLS
(JOSEPH WAS "TECHNOS")

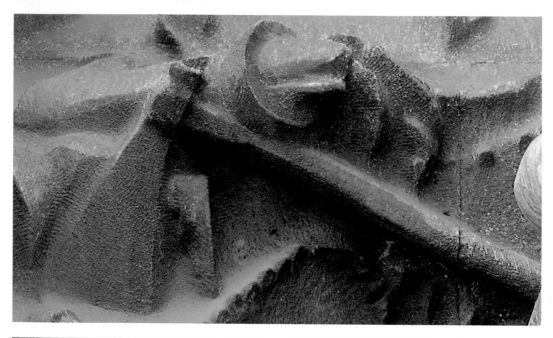

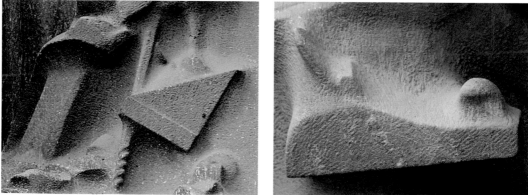

VARIOUS TOOLS: AXE, CARPENTER'S SQUARE, CARPENTER'S BRUSH... | GROUP FROM THE FLIGHT TO EGYPT PRODUCED BY LLORENÇ MATAMALA

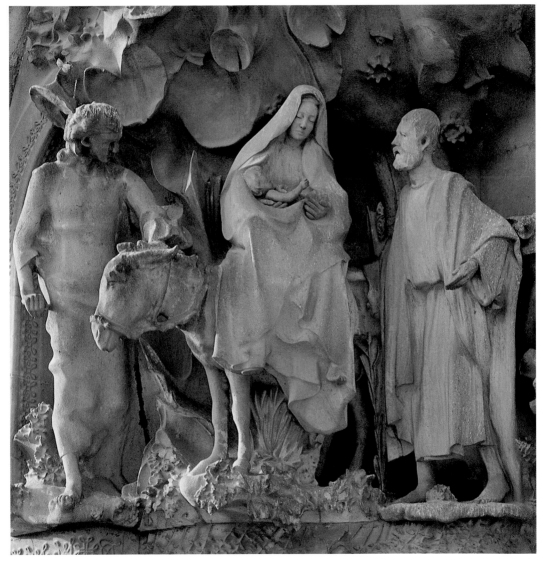

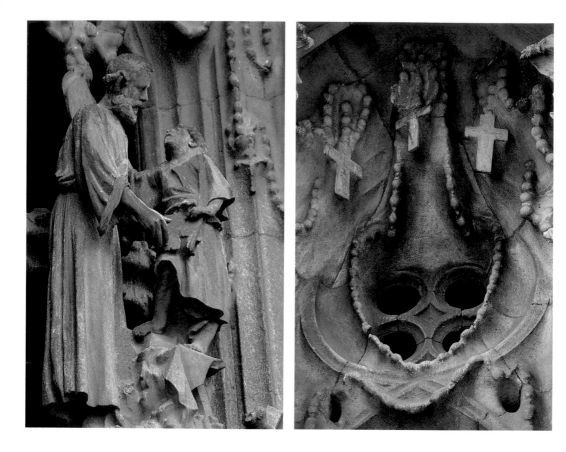

SAINT JOSEPH WITH THE BABY JESUS | ROSARY THAT FRAMES THE HOPE DOORWAY

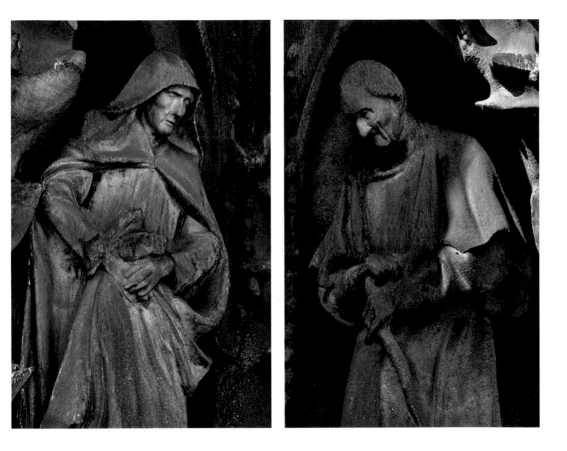

SAINT ANN AND SAINT JOACHIM, MARY'S PARENTS AND JESUS' GRANDPARENTS

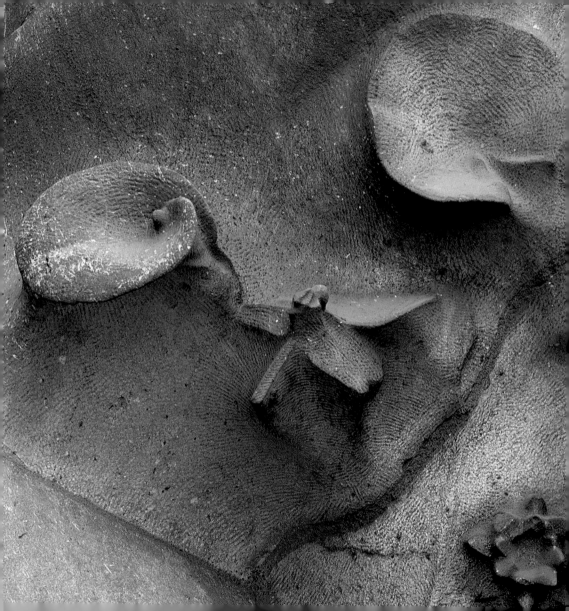

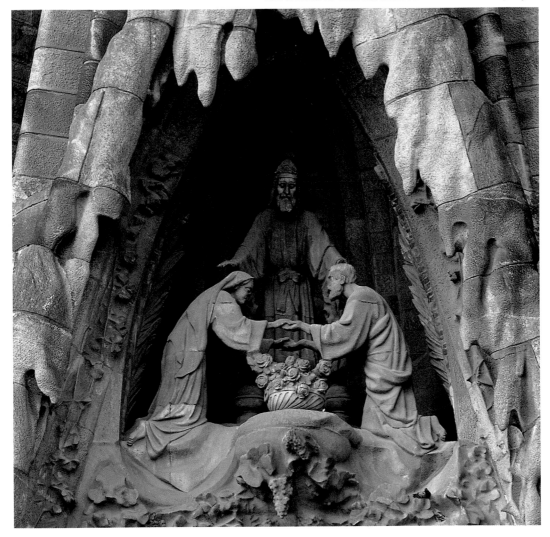

BETROTHAL OF THE VIRGIN AND SAINT JOSEPH

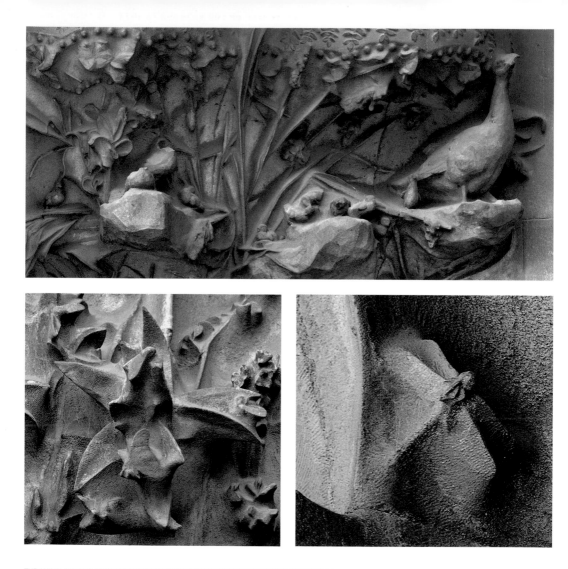

THE ANIMALS AND PLANTS THAT DECORATE THE HOPE DOORWAY CORRESPOND TO THE FLORA AND FAUNA OF THE NILE: WATER LILIES, DRAGONFLIES, ACACIAS...

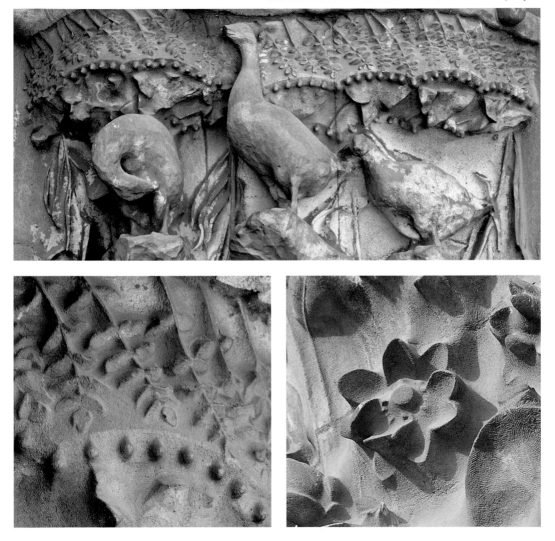

THE BOULDER OF MONTSERRAT,
WITH THE INSCRIPTION
"SAVE US" FLANKED BY THE
APOSTLES BARNABUS AND
SIMON. SHELTERED BELOW
THE ROCK IS THE BOAT
STEERED BY SAINT JOSEPH
—

THIS SAINT JOSEPH, POSITIONED
AFTER 1926, BEARS A CERTAIN
RESEMBLANCE TO GAUDÍ,
SOMETHING THAT COULD BE
INTERPRETED AS A POSTHUMOUS
HOMAGE TO THE ARCHITECT
BY THE TEMPLE WORKERS

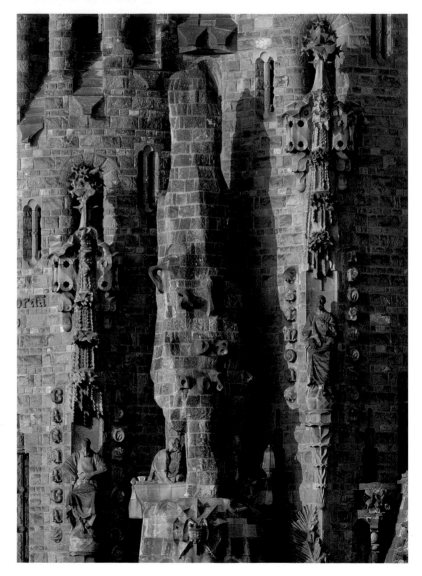

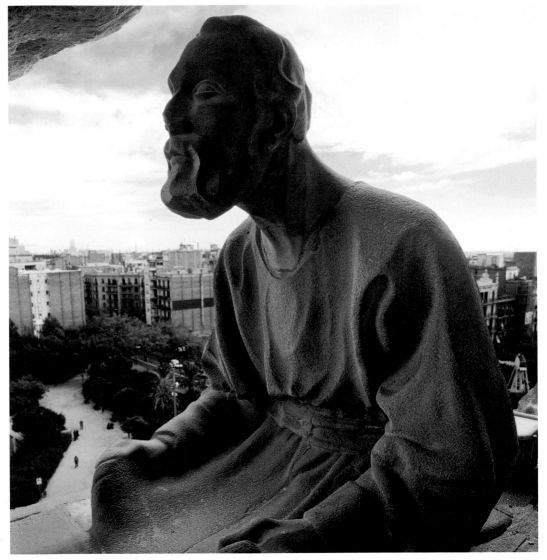

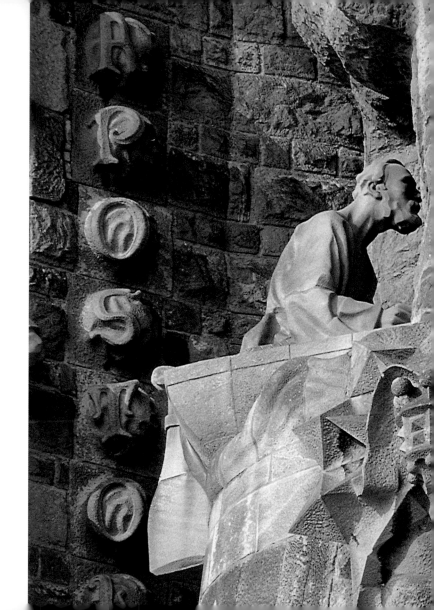

SAINT JOSEPH, CHOSEN
AS PATRON SAINT OF THE
UNIVERSAL CHURCH IN 1870,
STEERS THE CHURCH BOAT

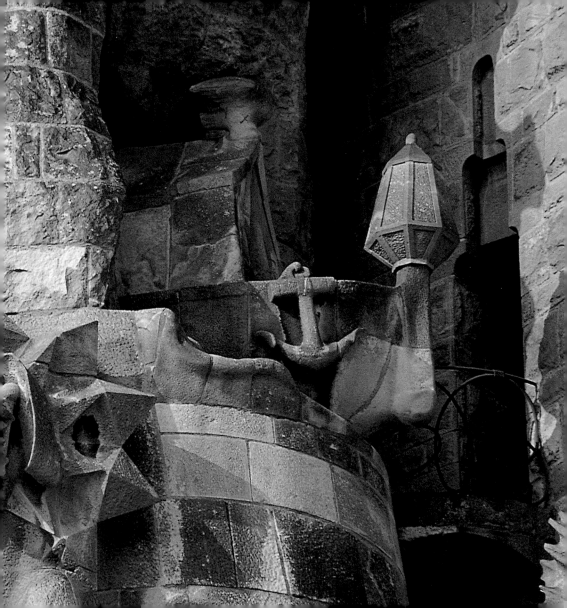

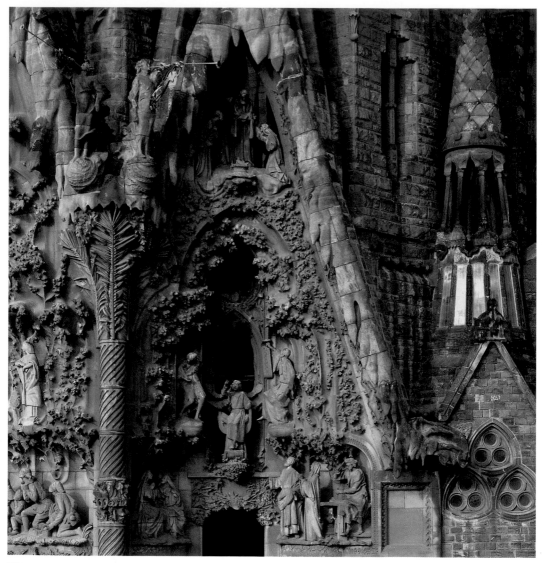

Faith Doorway

The portal on the right is the Faith Doorway, with illustrations of some passages from the Gospel and the major dogmas of the church of Rome, all relating to this theological virtue.

Amidst the different sculptured figures and groups there can be seen the Sacred Heart, starkly realistic, pierced with thorns, with flowers and bees that sip the divine blood. Above are various groups: the Visitation by Mary to her cousin Elizabeth; the house in Nazareth, where Jesus worked as a carpenter; Joseph and Mary gazing admiringly at Jesus, who shows signs of his divinity; Zachariah the priest, writing the name of John on the wall, after the angel announced to him that his wife was with child. Opposite is John the Baptist himself as a child, Jesus' cousin. And, on the atrium, the sculptural group repre-

BEE, SYMBOL OF
VIRGINAL SOULS

senting Jesus being presented in the temple. The upper levels represent the great, fundamental statements of Catholicism. The lamp represents the Trinity –Father, Son and Holy Ghost– and for that reason has a triple wick. Next, the Immaculate Conception, a dogma that was given renewed emphasis in Gaudí's time, and whose formulation tends to be forgotten. Mary had been conceived virginally by her own mother, Saint Ann, hence the declaration of faith: "Hail Mary, full of grace, conceived without sin". Next comes the Eucharist or Holy Communion, represented by bunches of grapes and ears of wheat. And finally the culmination: Divine Providence, as the supreme wisdom of God that governs and sustains the universe. This is denoted by an expressive symbol already used in Medieval churches: a hand with an eye set into it, representing God's care and foresight, which cares for all things and knows all things.

Although the details of the construction and architecture are the real basis of the Nativity Façade, it is the ornamentation, the sculpture and the corporeal symbols that are particularly striking for their spectacular profusion and exuberance.

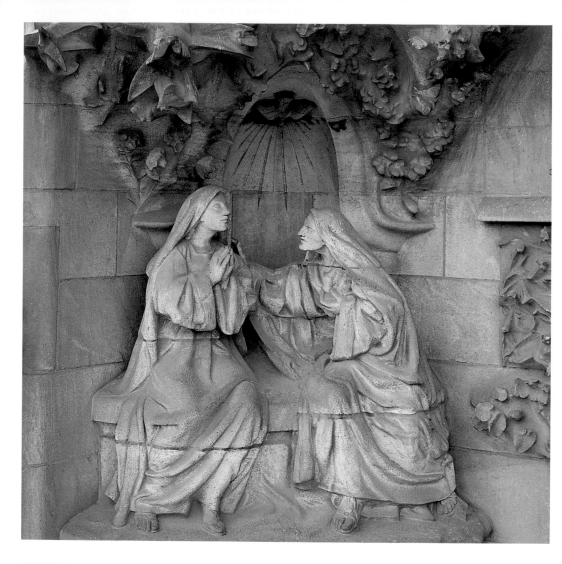

THE VISITATION: MARY ALONGSIDE ELIZABETH, THE MOTHER OF JOHN THE BAPTIST

Speaking of this, and in particular of the figures of animals, human beings, angels and divinities, it is worth remembering the following statement of Gaudí's, no doubt intended to provoke: "The most intense expression of a figure is given by its skeleton; all other things are details draped upon it, and many of these disappear when viewed from a distance." For that reason they had a jointed skeleton in the workshops, and hanging in the corners were dozens of wire or plaster figures, dressed or undressed, in various different sizes and ages. There was also a metal skeleton, which Gaudí carried around in his pocket.

Should we take it that the above-mentioned words from the maestro mean that structure is more important that ornament? And, furthermore that death is more certain and everlasting than life? At all events, his thought would not be complete without other utterances of his which suggest the opposite: decoration is what most strongly attracts one's attention, and that life, both this one and our eternal life, is the deepest and truest reality.

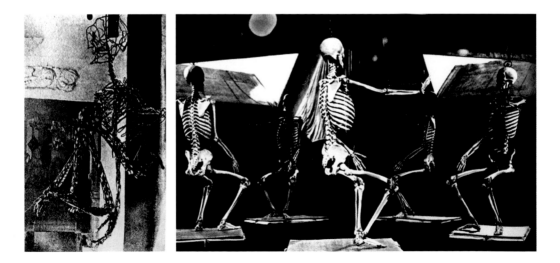

GAUDÍ STUDIED THE STRUCTURE OF SKELETONS IN GREAT DETAIL BECAUSE HE BELIEVED THAT THIS GAVE A FIGURE ITS REAL EXPRESSION

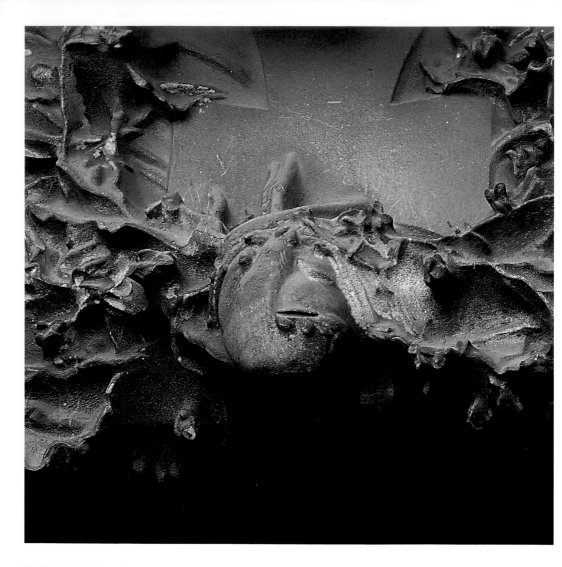

THE HEART OF JESUS IN THE LINTEL OF THE ENTRANCE

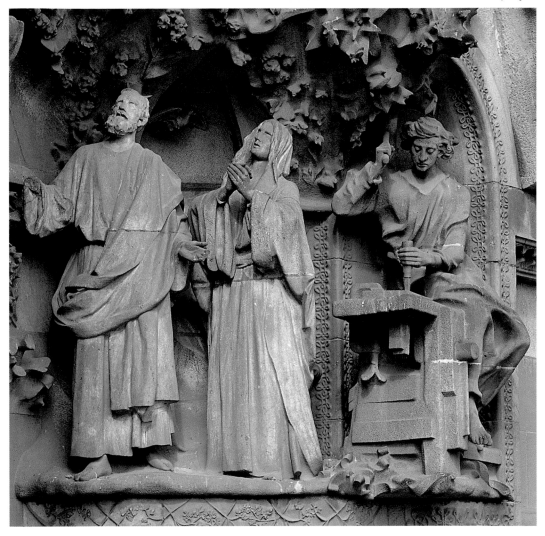

JESUS WORKING IN THE WORKSHOP OF NAZARETH. ABOVE HIS HEAD APPEARS A SYMBOLIC WORKER BEE

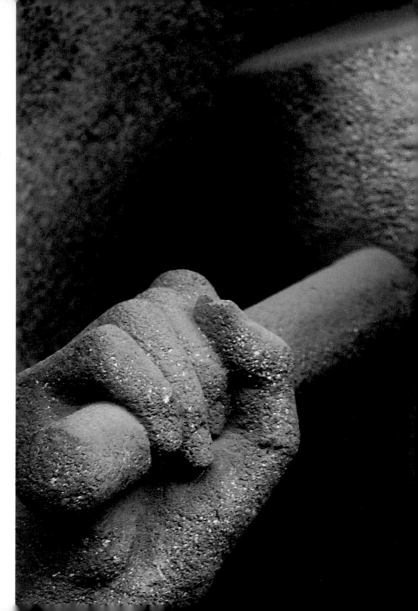

THIS WORKER JESUS, WORKING
HUMBLY IN HIS FATHER'S
WORKSHOP, RESPONDS TO GAUDÍ'S
DESIRE TO HIGHLIGHT THE EFFORT
OF WORK AS A PATH TO FOLLOW

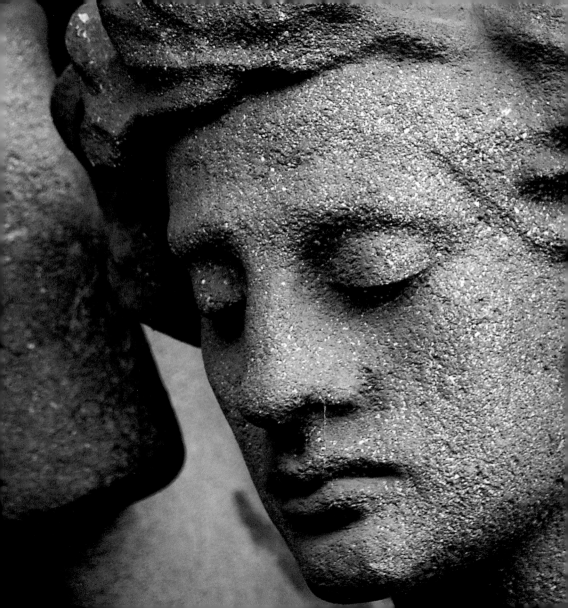

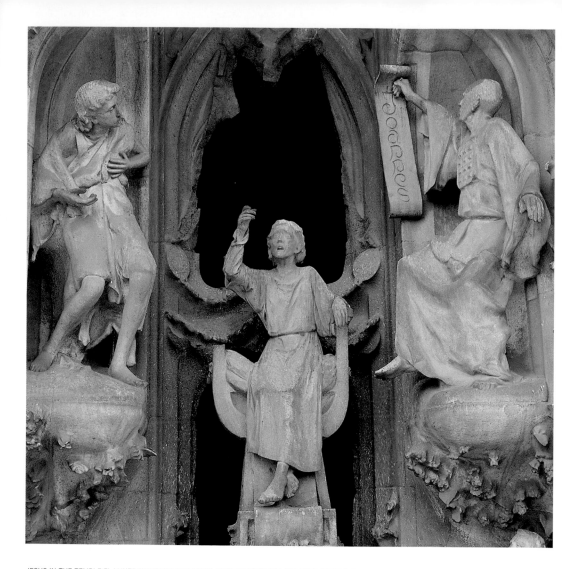

JESUS IN THE TEMPLE FLANKED BY HIS COUSIN SAINT JOHN THE BAPTIST AND THE LATTER'S FATHER, THE PRIEST ZACHARIAH

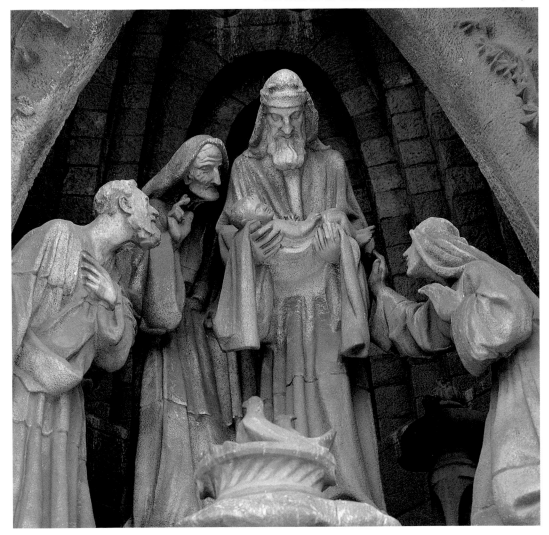

JESUS, IN THE ARMS OF SIMEON, IS PRESENTED IN THE TEMPLE BEFORE HIS PARENTS AND THE PROPHETESS ANNA. AT THEIR FEET THE TWO TURTLEDOVES OF THE SACRIFICE

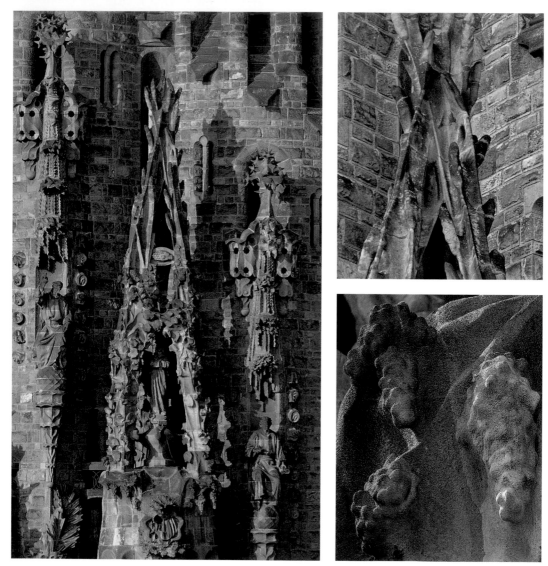

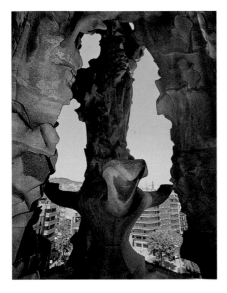

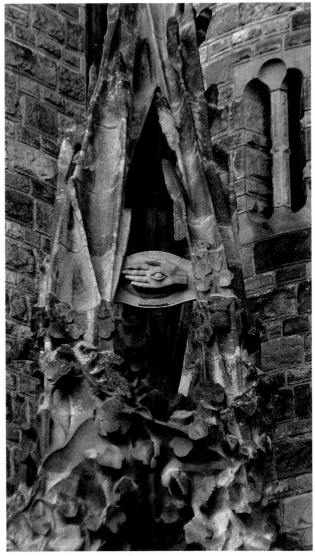

THE IMMACULATE CONCEPTION
SURROUNDED BY THE EUCHARISTIC
WHEATEARS AND VINE

THE THREE-ARMED CANDELABRA,
SYMBOL OF THE TRINITY AND THE
DIVINE PROVIDENCE, REPRESENTED
BY THE HAND WITH THE EYE

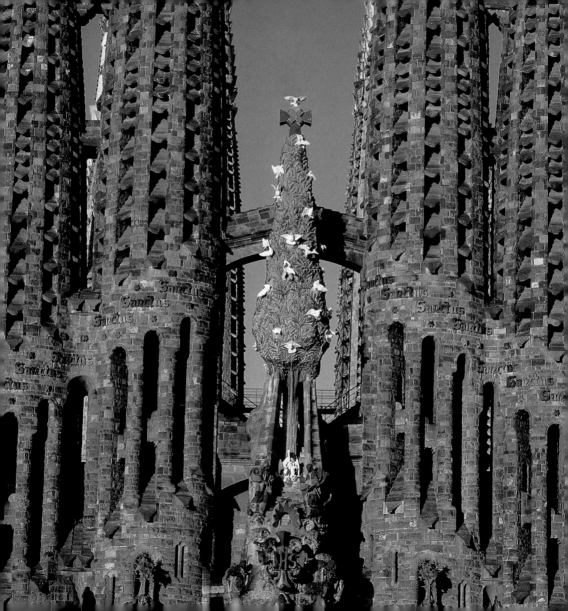

The Tree of Life

High up on the Nativity Façade is the spire representing a cypress tree that crowns the three portals of Faith, Hope and Charity.

But first, it should be noted that above the cave of the Virgin's Coronation, covered in snow falling in the shape of great floes, there is a complex and spectacular Jesus anagram. This has a cross at its centre, flanked by the "A" and "Ω", letters that signify the beginning and end of all things, that is, the cross as the origin and culmination of life and the universe.

A little higher up, there is an egg –quite visible but seldom remarked upon. This is a glass egg, golden and red in colour, which bears the JHS anagram of Jesus. This, probably, is the egg as the origin and fullness of the universe, as is the "dancing egg" over the fountain in the cloister of Barcelona Cathedral.

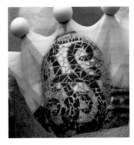

EGG WITH THE
ANAGRAM OF JESUS

The pelican that can be seen above it belongs to Christianity's primitive iconography, and indeed to earlier mythologies. The pelican myth contains the idea that this bird scratches its fish-replete belly with its beak, to give food and drink to its two little ones. For that reason it is used as a symbol of the Host and, on occasions, to represent the Resurrection.

Crowning the Nativity entrance is another symbolic representation: the cypress, the sign of that which is incorruptible. On either side, angels catch the Divine Blood in chalices to sprinkle over all the Earth, hence the large surrounding area with drops clinging to the stone. Other angels burn incense and sing hosanna and a further two, one with an amphora and the other with a basket of loaves, clearly represent the Eucharist (according to Cesar Martinell). The ladders that reach the highest point of the cypress perhaps signify the mystic aspiration to ascend to the very bosom of God, linked to the ascetic suffering represented by the strenuous effort needed to ascend such steep ladders.

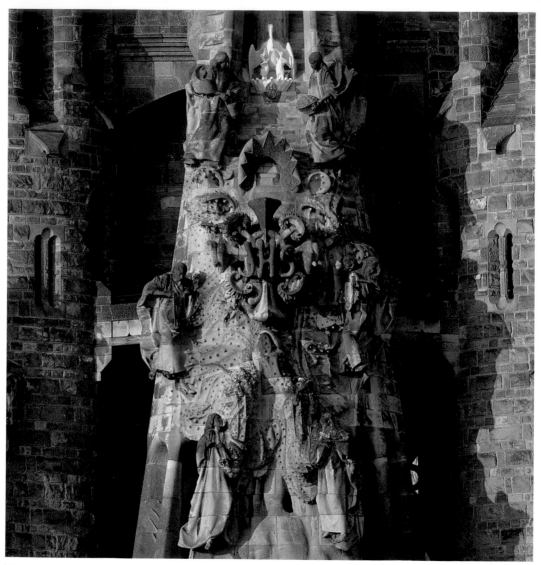

The previously-mentioned cypress is the Tree of Life everlasting, and is a refuge for the many alabaster doves taken from the iconography of primitive Christianity. Gaudí took as his model for the cypress one that was growing in the Carthusian monastery of Montalegre (in Tiana, not far from Barcelona) which would suggest that he was thinking of the life of the recluse typical of this monastery and which so attracted him.

At the top of the cypress tree is a letter T, or Tau, the first letter of the word God in Greek, and the last letter of the Hebrew alphabet; it is red in colour and crossed by two golden bars that form an X, on which is superimposed a dove with spread wings. The Tau, the X and the Dove represent the three persons of the Holy Trinity.

As for the bridge that lies behind the great cypress, it will be remembered that there are many such bridges flying from tower to tower in certain cathedrals. Gaudí said on one occasion that, "the Church is always building itself; the directors of works are the Pontifices –from Latin *ponti fex* which literally means to build bridges. And (the Church) is constantly creating its churches, its bridges to Glory". This is, in effect, the hidden symbolism of the bridge: to go from the depths to the heights, from the Here to the Beyond.

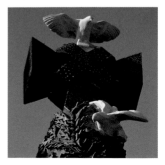

SCULPTURAL GROUP COMPRISING
THE PELICAN, WITH TWO ANGELS
CARRYING THE TRANSUBSTANTIATED
BREAD AND WINE, AND THE
ANAGRAM OF JESUS SURROUNDED
BY FOUR ANGELS WITH CENSERS

—

ON THE TOP OF THE TREE OF
LIFE, THE TAU, THE X AND THE
DOVE REPRESENT THE THREE
PERSONS OF THE TRINITY

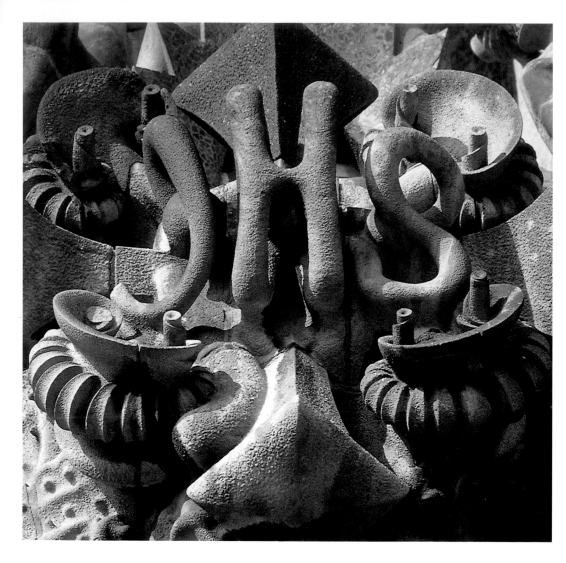

ANAGRAM OF JESUS

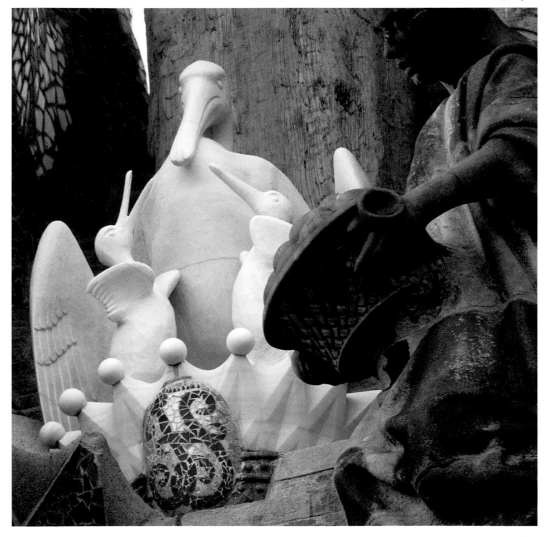

THE PELICAN, SYMBOL OF THE EUCHARIST

TO PRODUCE THIS TREE THAT
CROWNS THE NATIVITY FAÇADE,
GAUDÍ USED A CYPRESS
TREE FROM THE CARTHUSIAN
MONASTERY OF MONTEALEGRE
IN TIANA AS THE MODEL. THE
CYPRESS REPRESENTS IMMORTAL
LIFE AND THE INCORRUPTIBLE.
FLYING TOWARDS IT IN THE FORM
OF WHITE DOVES ARE THE PURE
SOULS THAT WAIT TO ENTER
PARADISE. CROWNED BY THE
GREEK LETTER TAU, THE X AND
THE DOVE -IN REFERENCE TO THE
THREE PERSONS OF THE TRINITY-,
THIS TREE IS THE THRESHOLD
THAT JOINS HEAVEN AND EARTH

—

THE BRIDGE CROSSING THE
CYPRESS TREE REFERS TO
THE COAT OF ARMS OF LEO
XIII, POPE OF THE CATHOLIC
CHURCH FROM 1878 UNTIL 1903

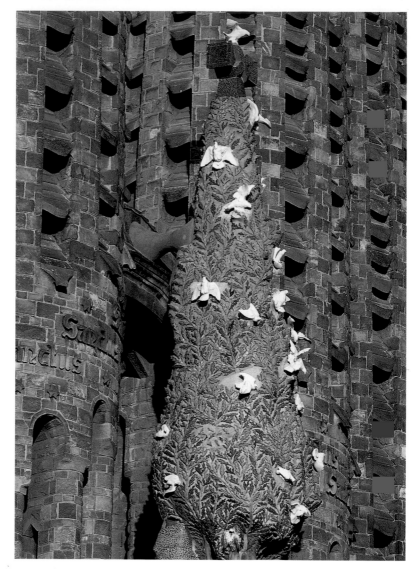

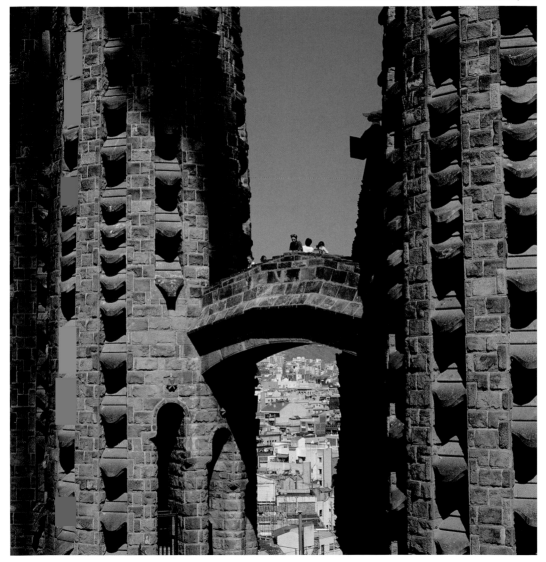

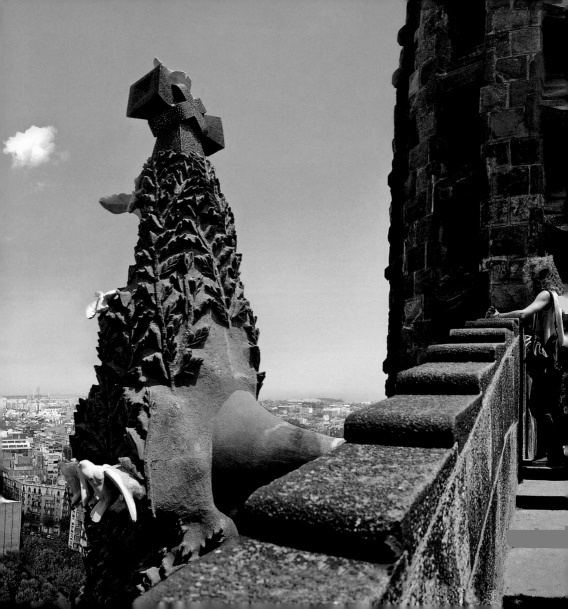

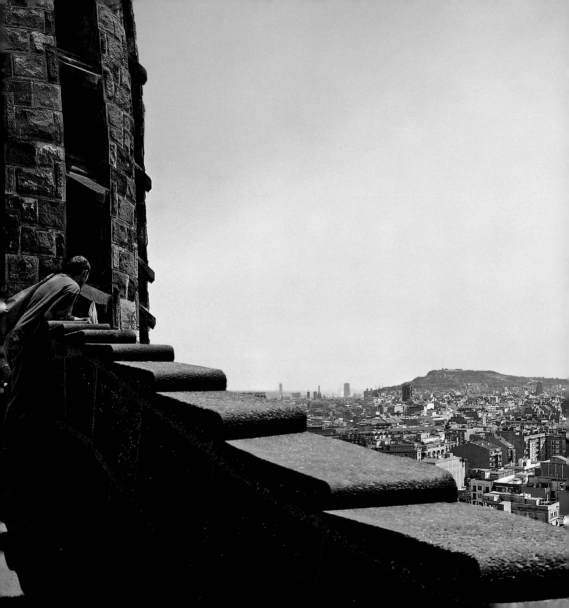

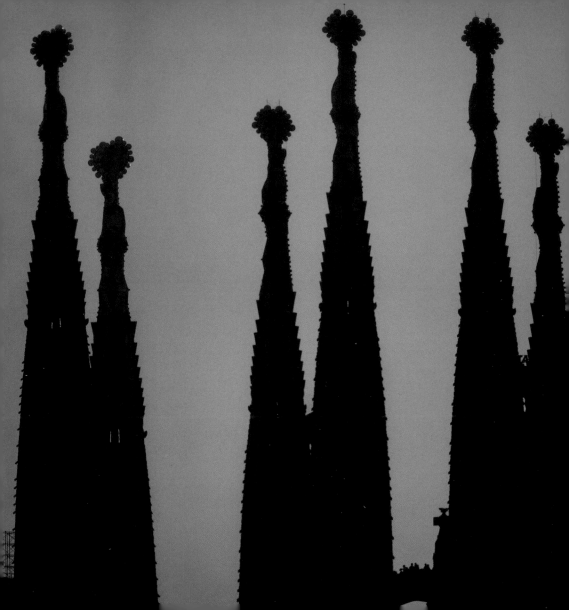

The Towers

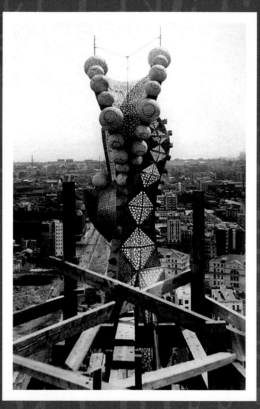

PINNACLE OF THE FIRST FINISHED TOWER DEDICATED TO SAINT BARNABUS (1925)

←

THE DUSK LIGHT SILHOUETTES THE OUTLINES OF THE TOWERS

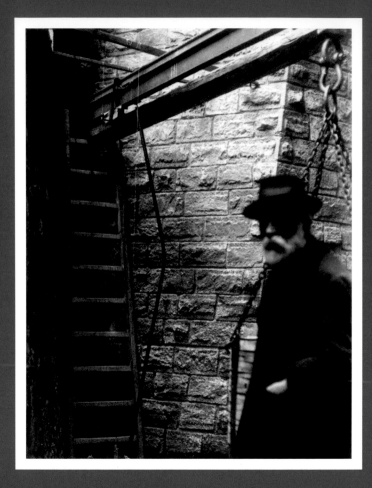

GAUDÍ OVERSEEING A RESISTANCE TEST OF MATERIALS FOR THE TEMPLE

The Towers

On 30th November 1925, the Saint Barnabas tower was topped out, the first on the left on the Nativity Façade. This was the only one that Gaudí lived to see finished, since he died a few months later. After so much work, difficulties and delays, this must have been a deeply satisfying moment: he could now experience for himself the attractiveness of this highly elaborate work, and he at last had a finished sample of his cathedral to show his compatriots. They could now look at this part and have a good idea of what the whole building would be like when completed.

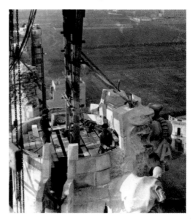

THE TOWERS OF THE NATIVITY FAÇADE UNDER CONSTRUCTION

The towers are as surprising inside as they are from the outside. To visit them one can use the stairs or the lift or combine both means of ascent. In the lower part of the towers there are spiral staircases which are so steep they scarcely have a rail. They spiral around a very narrow space, so those climbing them get the impression they are rotating upon themselves. In fact, the optical effect of looking at these stairs from top to bottom, or from the bottom to the top, is one of the indelible impressions left by the visit. Furthermore, the stairs in some towers spiral one way, and their twins spiral in the opposite direction, which increases the sensory richness.

When the top of the rectangular tower is reached, it is possible to go from this tower to the neighbouring one, through what is an extraordinary vertical labyrinth. Inside one of the four towers is a lift, taking visitors from the ground to the area where the wall with slatted shutters begins. Here the stairs are supported by the outside walls.

The upper part of the towers is where the bells will be hung in the final stages of construction. Also, within the square base and the surrounding façade there are several galleries one above the other which can be seen from inside the church: during services some of the congregation will be able to occupy them.

One of Gaudí's great passions was music, as can be seen in many of the details of his buildings. On the subject of bells for the Sagrada Familia, he said (according to César Martinell) that there were basically three kinds: the ordinary ones; those tuned to the notes mi, sol, do, which are the easiest notes to obtain with this type, and tubular bells, which are made to sound by percussion or by passing air through them. These last produce all notes and can be played like a piano or a harmonium.

Around 1915 Gaudí carried out many tests with different types of bells. He had several books sent from abroad on the subject, although he typically preferred to make the bells based on the experience he continued acquiring as he got to know them and their notes thoroughly. The Liceu Opera House loaned him several instruments, including a harmonium and a violin, and he regularly carried a book around with him containing notes and drawings on the questions he was studying.

Among the numerous observations he jotted down are the following:

"When the weather is damp the sound of bells carries much less, despite the fact that, according to Physics, dampness is a good conductor of sound. The older the bells are, the better they sound. They continue to improve until the day before they crack, which is when they are at their best. The melancholy sound of bells at the close of day arises from the harmony between the dying day and voice of the bronze, the latter growing ever more expressive as it nears its end".

When the first tower was finished, the clockmaker who looked after the running of the three clocks of the Sagrada Familia exclaimed: "Now I've seen the tower finished! *Fa goig*! (It looks good!)." Gaudí was highly pleased by this opinion, because it came from a simple man who saw the completion of something he perhaps thought he would not see in his lifetime, but also because the Catalan idiom, *fa goig*, is an expression that captures more accurately than most the surprise and the joy that something produces, whether it be a table spread with good food, a beautiful woman or a work of art such as this.

In the years that followed, the architect Sugrañes, Gaudí's successor in charge of the project, completed the other three towers; subsequently the four towers of the Passion Façade were put up, almost identical to the first, finishing in 1977. And it will be several years before the four Glory towers, considerably higher than the rest, are completed.

The towers are dedicated to the twelve apostles. The four oldest –94 metres high on the outside and 107 metres on the inside– are adorned with the respective names and statues of the apostles Barnabas, Simon, Judas Thaddaeus and Mathew, all of them seated on pedestals, with the inscription *Sursum corda* (Lift up your hearts, in Latin). After the death of Jesus, Mathew was chosen to replace Judas Iscariot. John the Evangelist instead of having an apostle tower dedicated to him will have one of the Evangelist towers –since he was both an apostle and one of the four writers of the Gospels. These are situated over the central nave.

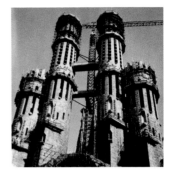

CONSTRUCTION OF THE PASSION
TOWERS (APPROX. 1973)

An unusual feature is that one of the towers is rectangular at the base, and from the height of the façade upwards (a quarter of the total height) becomes circular in section. There are many ecclesiastical buildings with towers that have a square base, and few that have a round base, but there are none that combine both patterns. However, the central salon in the Palau Güell, also in Barcelona, has a square base and above it a circular dome that stands out surprisingly from the rest of the building. In the case of the Sagrada Familia, the rectangular structure is transformed (by architectural sleight of hand) into a tubular shape, just where the statue of each apostle is positioned. Gaudí never explicitly explained why there is this change from the square to the circular, and commentators have limited themselves to saying that the change is very successful from the aesthetic point of view, which is certainly true.

Lower down, these four square towers have very rough, furrowed surfaces. On the next level, there are high, increasingly vertical columns, and higher up there is a combination of walls inset with slats, giving this section its characteristic look. The function of these slats is to send the sound of the bells from inside the belfry outward and downward to the ground and to the city beyond.

Up to this point, every one of the towers has its natural colour, the colour of the stone. Even so, the fact that the bell-towers are in pairs means that they throw long shadows which accentuate their respective volumes with light and shadow. This is one of the effects Gaudí most sought after in all his great architectural works.

On high, the pinnacles are formed by smooth or spherical surfaces which are marvellously complex, varied and alive. These terminals are 25 metres high, and they are a feast of colours, shapes and materials, symbols and originality. With these, Gaudí, entered into the realms of modern sculpture based on the liturgy. Indeed, these terminals represent the bishops, the apostles' successors, and for that reason they are the culmination and feature their attributes: the ring, the crosier, the mitre and the cross.

If we look from the base, we see, first of all, the words Hosanna and Excelsis framed in hexagons. Above these there are geometric shapes formed by gold and silver Venetian mosaics on a red background. At the highest level is the mitre or cap, with an opening in the middle, and with a sort of flower forming the apex that is more visible if viewed from the side. There is a red cross on each one of the two fanned-out faces. Each face has fifteen white balls, three large ones and twelve small ones. Below this, a not very visible truncated pyramid imitates the curvature of the crosier. The ring is below that. And finally, in the round mouths of the hexahedron there are a number of hollows that will be furnished with reflectors once the cathedral is finished. These will illuminate the towers and the façade from top to bottom. The pinnacles will be spectacular and visible from afar because of their colour and brilliance.

Gaudí did not like buildings to terminate in lightning conductors and such metallic objects: "The extremities of buildings with little metallic elements like crosses, weather vanes, and so forth, are like the bald lady with just one hair in the middle," he used to remark humorously. Actually, on one occasion when Gaudí was going up one the towers under construction, he slipped and almost fell to his death. After that the younger architects Rubió and Sugrañes took his place on any particularly hazardous task. Gaudí always said it was his patron saint Anthony of Padua who saved him. Although Gaudí also celebrated the feast of another Saint Anthony, it was the famous abbot and desert hermit, who in time began to interest Gaudí more, because of his life of solitude and sacrifice.

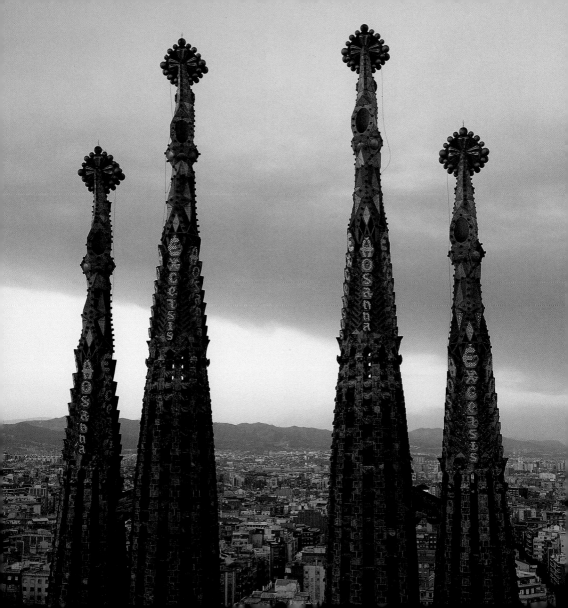

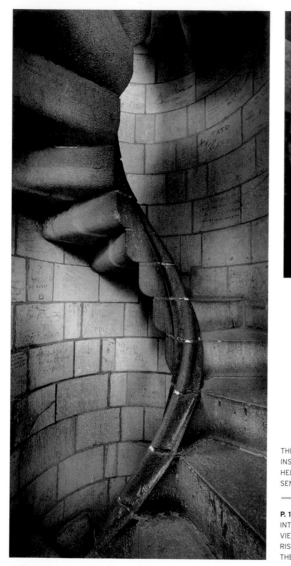

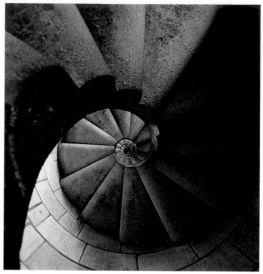

THE SPIRAL STAIRS ON THE
INSIDE OF THE TOWERS TURN
HELICOIDALLY, PRODUCING A DIZZYING
SENSATION OF MOVEMENT

—

P. 138-139
INTERIOR OF THE TOWERS AND
VIEW FROM THE WINDOWS WHICH
RISE HELICOIDALLY FOLLOWING
THE MOVEMENT OF THE STAIRS

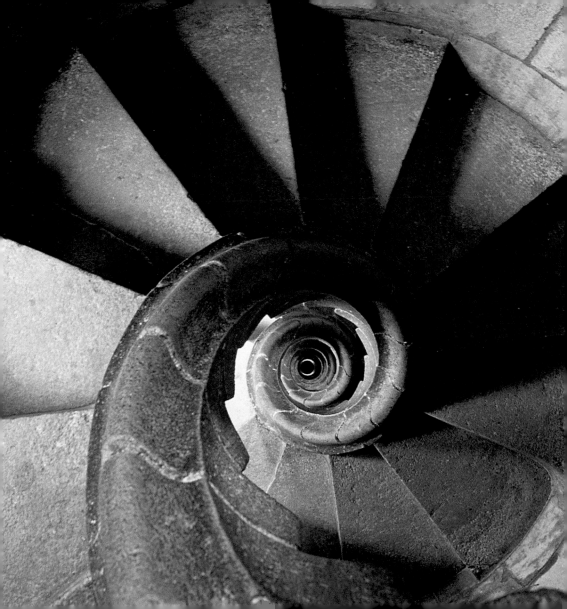

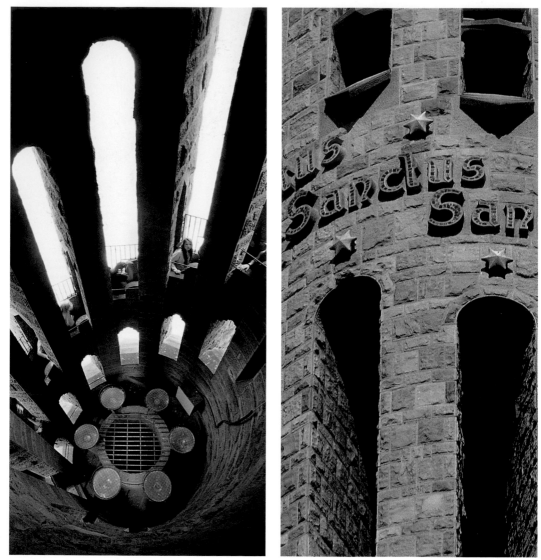

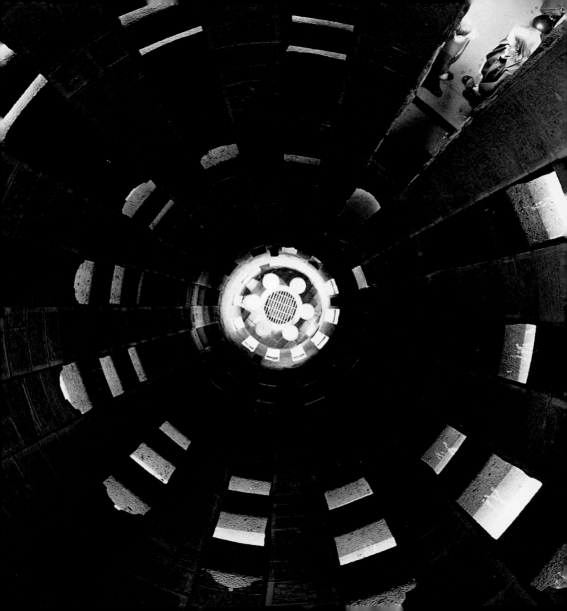

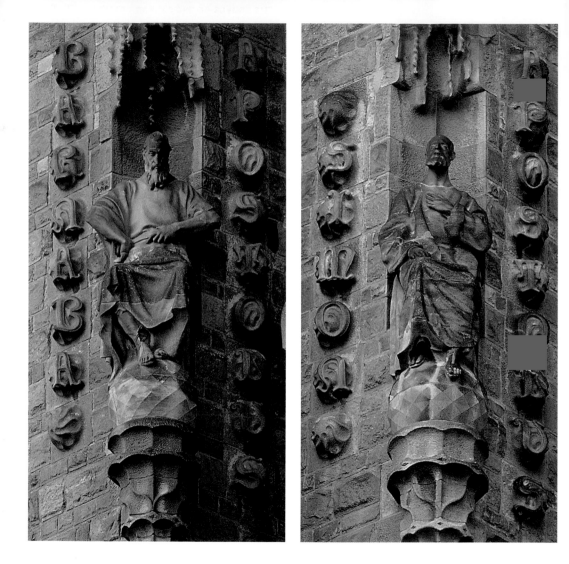

BARNABUS, SIMON, JUDAS AND MATTHEW, THE APOSTLES THAT PROVIDE THE NAMES FOR THE TOWERS ON THE NATIVITY FAÇADE

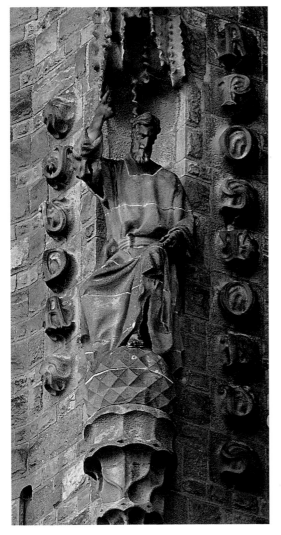

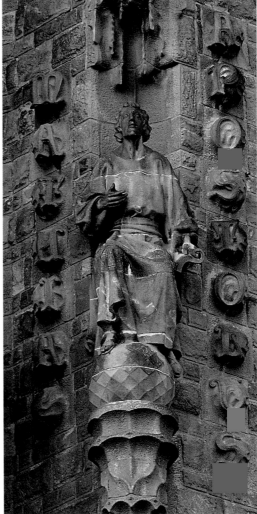

THESE FOUR FIGURES WERE SCULPTED BY LLORENÇ MATAMALA

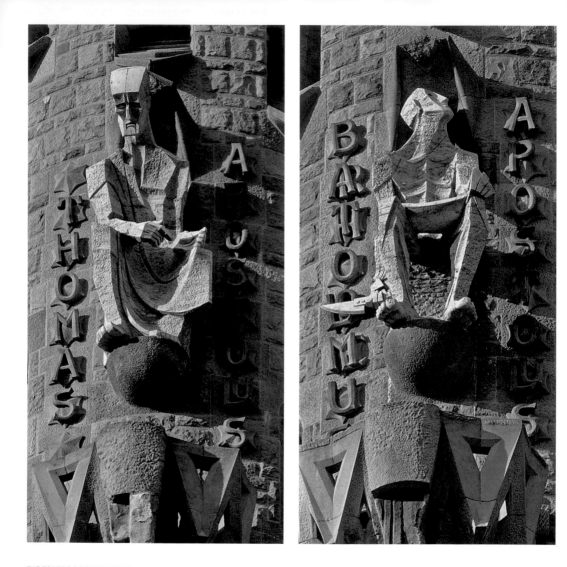

THE TOWERS OF THE PASSION FAÇADE ARE DEDICATED TO THE APOSTLES THOMAS, BARTHOLOMEW, JACOB AND PHILIP

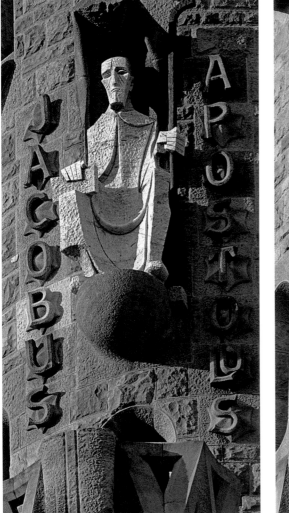

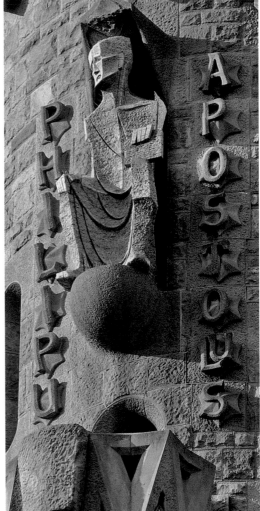

THE STYLISATION OF THESE FIGURES BY SUBIRACHS, LEANING TOWARDS ABSTRACTION, CONTRAST WITH THE FIGURATIVE STYLE OF THE APOSTLES ON THE NATIVITY FAÇADE

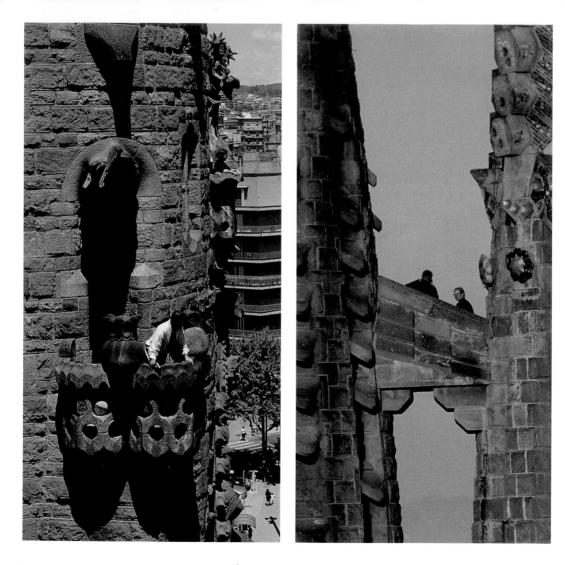

BALCONY WITH THE SYMBOLS OF JESUS, MARY AND JOSEPH | COMMUNICATING BRIDGE BETWEEN TWO TOWERS

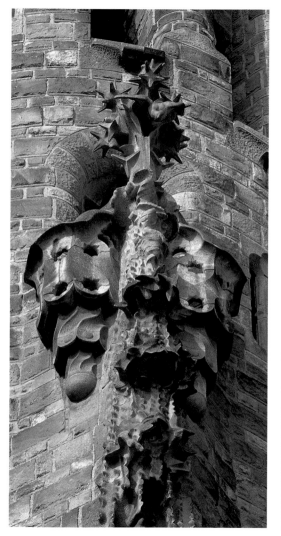

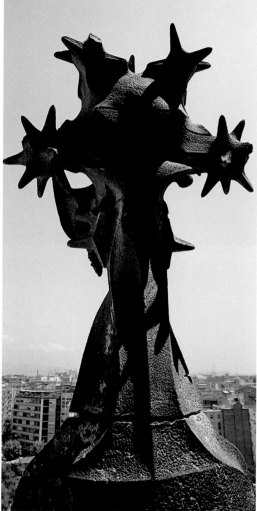

THESE BALCONIES, HALF WAY UP THE FAÇADE, ARE CRISS-CROSSED BY STARRY-SHAPED PINNACLES THAT CROWN THE NICHES OF THE APOSTLES. ALTOGETHER IT CREATES A VISUAL TRANSITION BETWEEN THE SQUARE GROUND PLAN OF THE TOWERS AND THEIR CIRCULAR UPPER SECTION

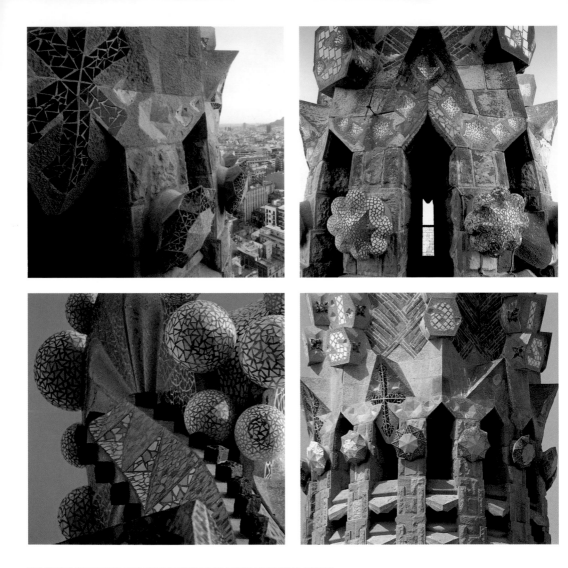

THE COLOUR ON THE HIGH PART OF THE TOWERS IS THE RESULT OF VENETIAN MOSAICS

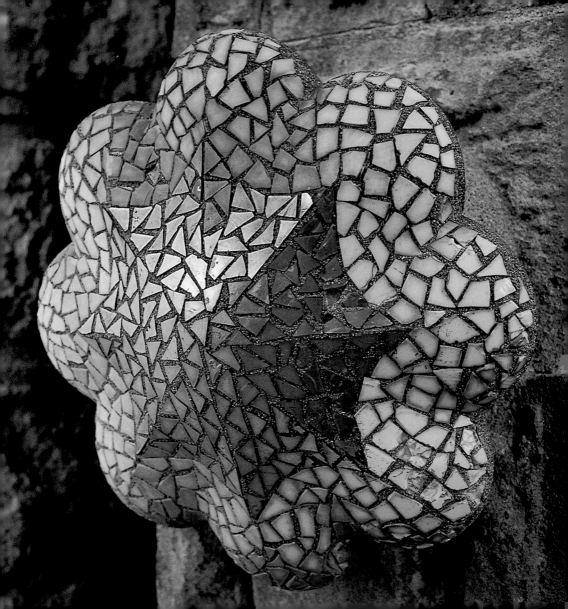

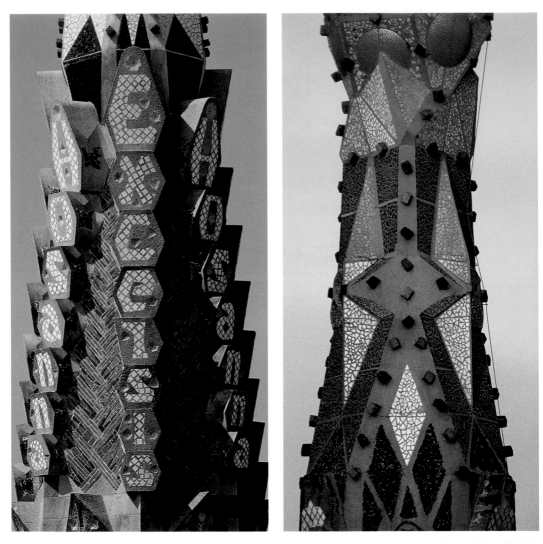

THE TWELVE BELL TOWERS OF THE TEMPLE ARE DEDICATED TO THE APOSTLES. THEIR PINNACLES TAKE THE FORM OF THE EPISCOPAL SIGNS OF AUTHORITY: THE TWO-POINTED PENTAGONAL MITRE, THE BISHOP'S STAFF IN THE FORM OF A HOOK THAT CROSSES THE MITRE, AND THE CROSS AND THE BISHOPS' RINGS.

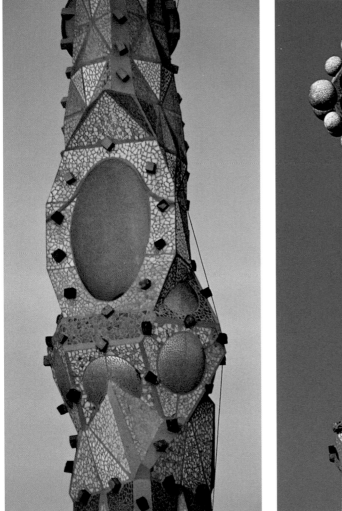
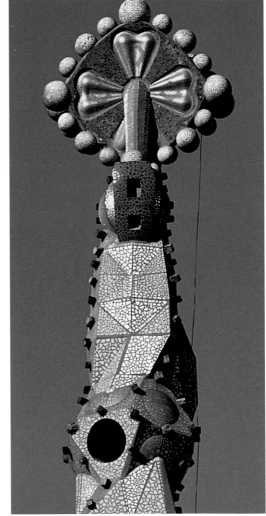

THE KNOT OF THE STAFF IS PERFORATED FOR POSITIONING THE REFLECTORS THAT
LIGHT UP THE CROSS OF THE CENTRAL DOME INSIDE THE TEMPLE AND THE CITY OUTSIDE

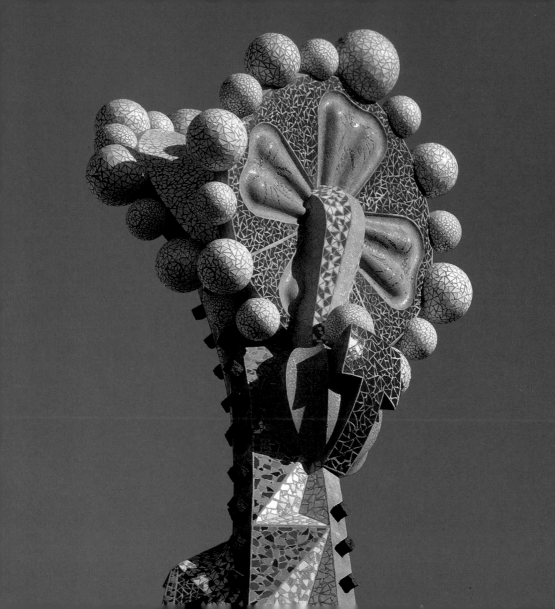

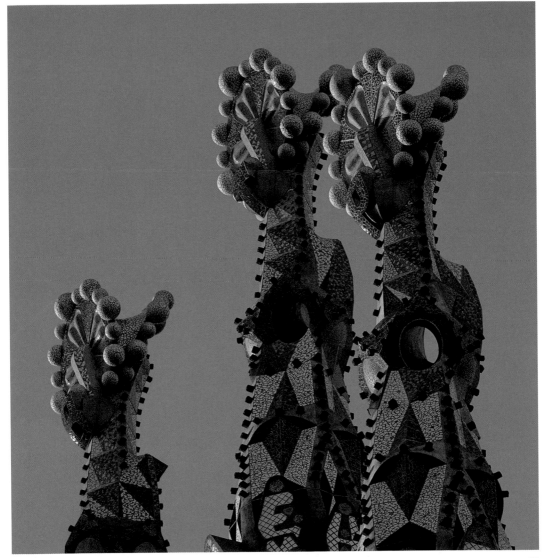

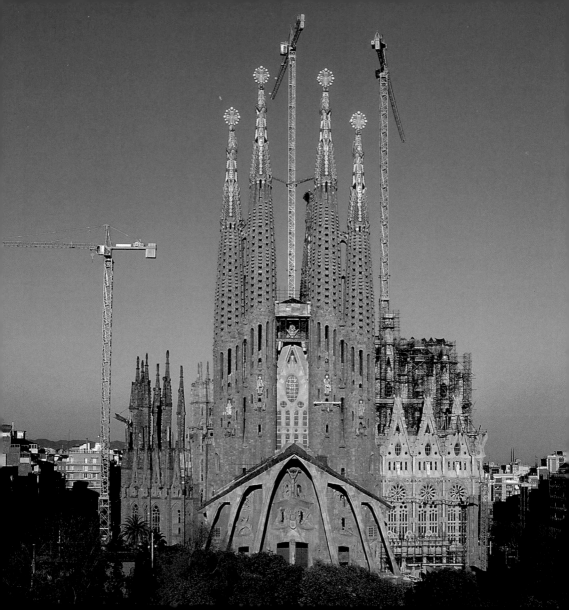

The Passion Façade

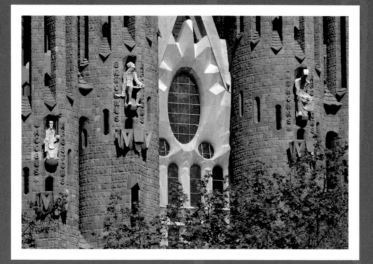

STAINED-GLASS WINDOW ON THE
PASSION FAÇADE
←
THE WESTERN OR PASSION FAÇADE

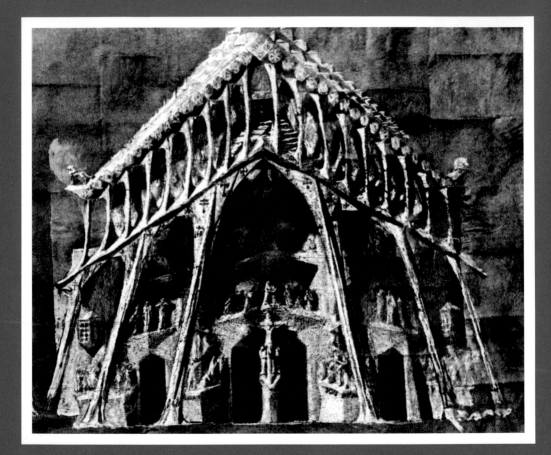

PROJECT FOR THE PASSION FAÇADE DRAWN BY GAUDÍ IN 1911

The Passion Façade

"If we had begun by building this façade, people would have backed out." This was the reason that Gaudí gave for not having begun the church with the Passion Façade. This in itself illustrates the dramatic impact that he wanted to have: he had thought much about how he wanted this side –more correctly called the Passion and Death Façade.

When he was ill in Puigcerdà on the French border in 1911 (and so convinced he was at death's door that he made his will) he drew a sketch of this entrance. The drawing has survived, and illustrates the last week in Christ's life. We can see from the drawing that it involves highly moving sculptures, reminiscent of the artists and sculptors of the expressionist school. Expressionism, of course, was one of Gaudí's favourite artistic movements, as is plain from the crypt of the Colonia Güell.

But what most impresses about this drawing is the atrium, consisting of columns that resemble bones and decidedly disturbing in their innovation and strength. "I am ready to sacrifice the construction, to break arches, cut columns, in order to give the idea that sacrifice is a bloody business" Gaudí once said.

He did not live long enough to be able to build this grim entrance, and in 1988 these sculptures were entrusted to the sculptor Josep Maria Subirachs. That the latter was perhaps the best-fitted artist at that point is shown by the following observations from the Catalan art scholar Cirici Pellicer. In his book *L'art català contemporani*, he writes: "(Subirachs) was creating singular sculpture that brings Gaudí to mind, in the typical violent position of those bringers-of-fire who come up against meanness."

Nevertheless, the appointing of Subirachs by the Board in charge of the works came under fire from the very first moment, creating one of the stormiest controversies ever in Catalonia. At all events, if the parts of the cathedral done by Gaudí are clearly differentiated from the rest, it seems legitimate that the work should continue, since Gaudí frequently insisted that absolutely everything should be completed.

There is no doubt that the construction of the new parts, created on the basis of somewhat battered and often provisional models, will result in architecture that is more Gaudian than Gaudí, so to speak.

But that is not really a serious problem, since most of us are not architects enough to be able to imagine clearly what the final result would be like. Various critics have said that if and when the cathedral is finished, it will be more grandiose and exuberant than any in Christendom.

What is more, as the Sagrada Familia is a religious building, it does not make sense to judge it solely from the artistic point of view. Religious and artistic dimensions are of equal importance.

Subirachs began work in 1989, after a year of immersing himself in Gaudí's architectural and sculptural work. On a sort of three-level stage, the sculptor presents the story of the Passion from the Last Supper to the Death. Subirachs plots out an order –in the form of an inverted S– in which to look at the figures, from the Last Supper to the Crucifixion and Burial. With this strange distribution, he argues there is no need to have the conventional order, taking a stance similar to Gaudí's, and invites us to look at the deep meaning frequently found in the unconventional.

The sculptures by Subirachs are typical of his style, with angles, lines, clear outlines, giving value to the volume of the clothing, and treating the bodies schematically. But at the same time he does not depart much from the details provided by Gaudí and his vision. Thus, the crown of thorns consists of Gaudian thorns; the Evangelist figure is taken directly from Gaudí; the warriors are taken with little change from the warriors on the roof of La Pedrera; the column that Jesus is tied to is an unstable one like some in the crypt of the Colonia Güell; the Alpha and Omega are as centrally important here as in the Colonia's crypt or indeed in the Nativity Façade of the cathedral, and so on.

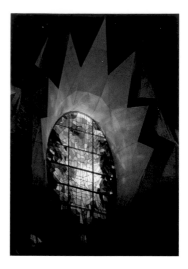

STAINED-GLASS WINDOW ON THE
PASSION FAÇADE

And Subirachs, too, poses riddles, as Gaudí does in a number of his works. The magic square that Subirachs places next to Judas' kiss is a cryptogram, the sum of whose combinations is always 33, Christ's age when he died; although there are other more or less esoteric readings.

As a plastic artist, Josep María Subirachs succeeds sculptor Lorenzo Matamala, his son Juan, Carlos Mani and Ricardo Opisso, all contemporaries of Gaudí, as well as Jaime Busquets and Japanese Etsuro Sotoo, the last-mentioned still actively engaged on the project.

Of all the elements that make up the Sagrada Familia, the architectural, the ornamental and the pictorial, the sculptures have been the most controversial and problematic from the start.

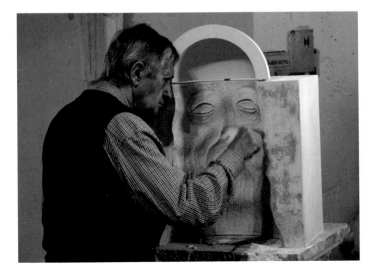

THE SCULPTOR JOSEP MARIA SUBIRACHS (11-03-1927) HAS WORKED ON THE PASSION FAÇADE SINCE 1987. THE ARTIST HAS DEVELOPED A NEO-FIGURATIVE LANGUAGE IN WHICH THE FRONTIER BETWEEN FORM AND ABSTRACTION BLEND TOGETHER IN A DISCOURSE THAT JOINS OPPOSITES: POSITIVE AND NEGATIVE, CONCAVE AND CONVEX, FULL AND EMPTY... THE SCULPTURES HAVE A STRONG, ALMOST VIOLENT, DRAMATIC NATURE AND A TRAGIC EXPRESSIVENESS IN LINE WITH THE SUBJECT MATTER THEY DEAL WITH: THE DEATH OF CHRIST

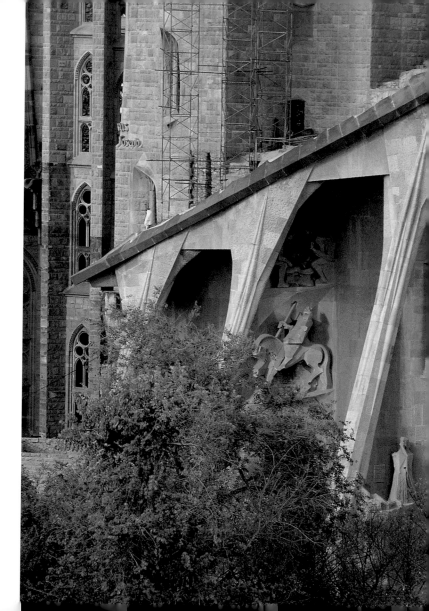

THE DIFFERENT SCENES ARE
POSITIONED RISING IN THE
FORM OF AN S

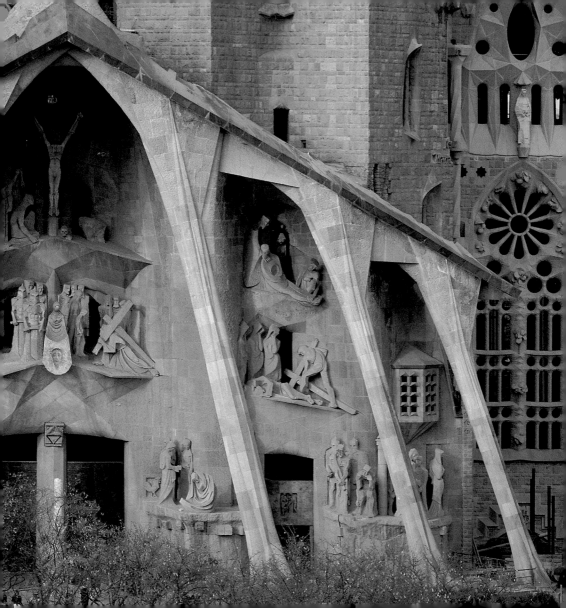

THIS FIGURE SHOWS A
SORROWFUL JESUS THE
MOMENT HE ANNOUNCES TO
HIS FOLLOWERS THAT ONE OF
THEM IS GOING TO BETRAY HIM

—

PREPARATORY DRAWING AND
SCULPTURE OF THE GROUP OF
THE LAST SUPPER OF JESUS
WITH THE TWELVE APOSTLES

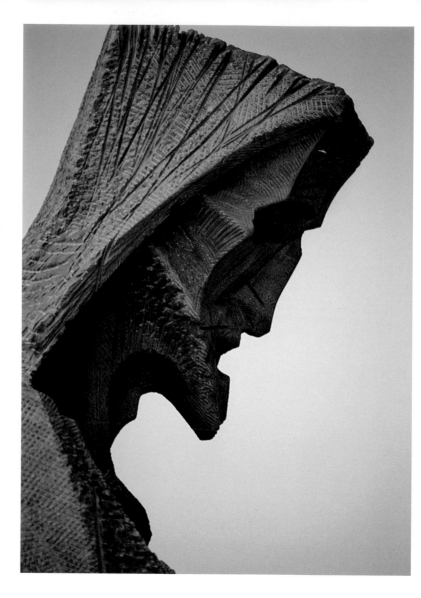

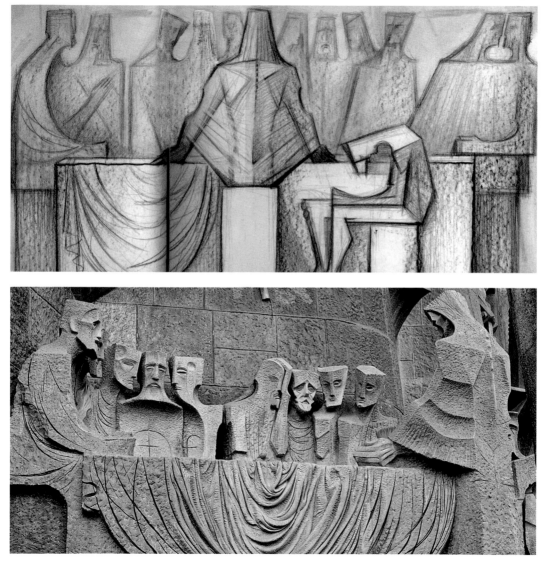

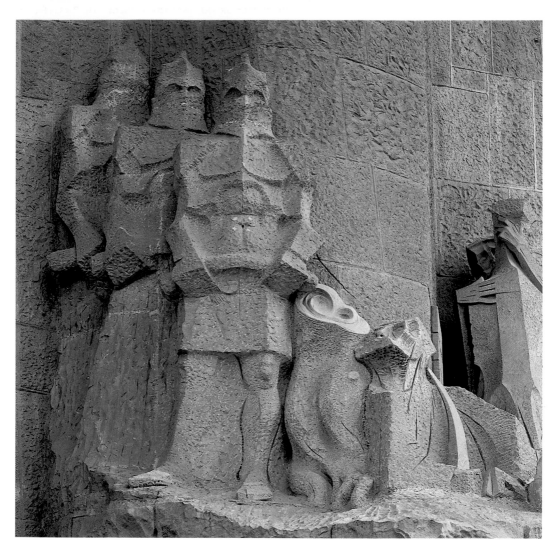

BETWEEN PETER AND THE GROUP OF SOLDIERS CAN BE SEEN A CUT TRUNK OF AN OLIVE TREE AND THE WOOD GRAIN GIVES A HINT OF THE EAR OF MALCHUS, THE HIGH PRIEST'S SERVANT, THAT PETER CUT OFF

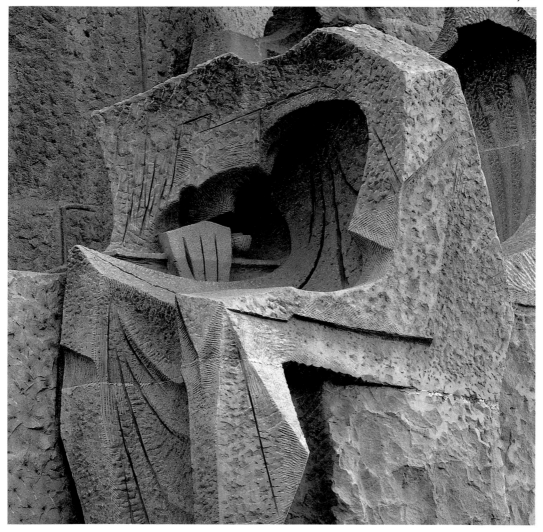

THE FIGURE OF SAINT JOHN EXPRESSES DEEP SORROW

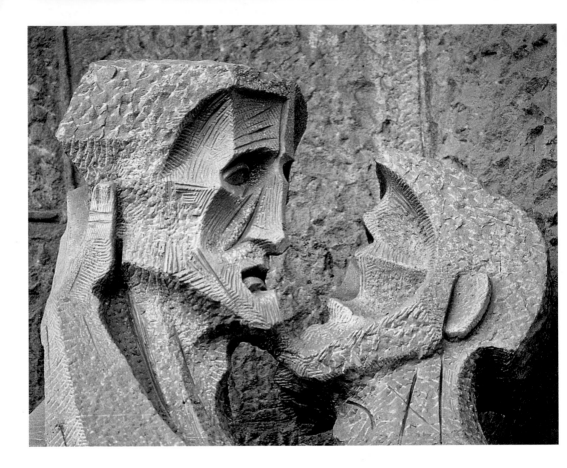

THE SCULPTURE OF JESUS, STIFF AND DISTANT, RECEIVES THE FALSE KISS FROM THE TRAITOR JUDAS WHO ACTS ENCOURAGED BY THE DEVIL IN THE FORM OF A SNAKE

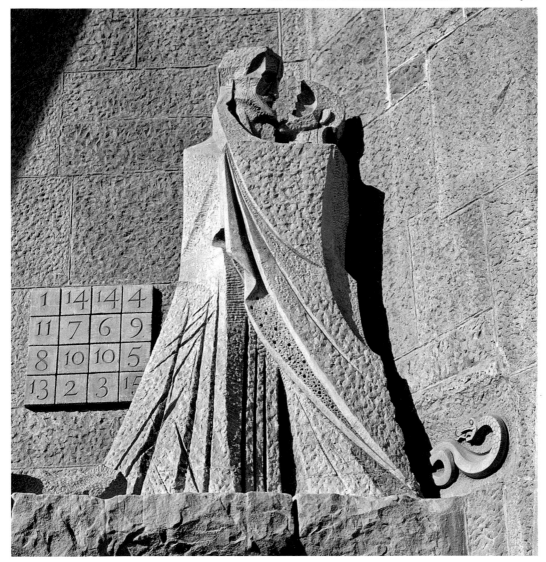

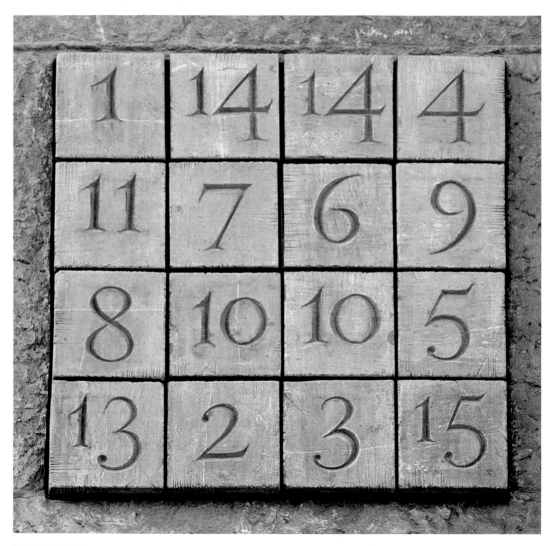

FROM THE CRYPTOGRAM, AN ENIGMATIC TABLE WITH 16 FIGURES, 310 COMBINATIONS CAN BE MADE THAT ALWAYS ADD UP TO 33, CHRIST'S AGE WHEN HE DIED | THE DOG, SYMBOL OF LOYALTY, AND THE SNAKE, SYMBOL OF TEMPTATION

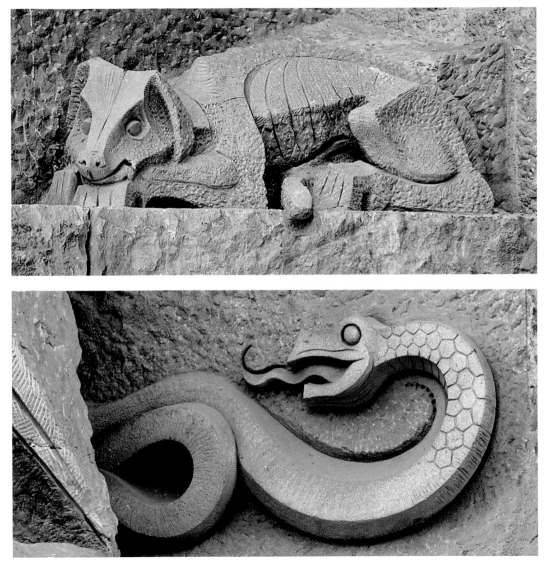

IN THE SCULPTURE OF THE
FLAGELLATION, JESUS APPEARS
TIED TO A COLUMN DIVIDED INTO
FOUR PARTS WHICH SYMBOLISE
THE FOUR ARMS OF THE CROSS
AND THE COLLAPSE OF THE
ANCIENT WORLD. THE THREE
STEPS THAT LEAD TO THE COLUMN
REPRESENT THE DAYS OF PASSION
AND DEATH THAT PRECEDED
CHRIST'S RESURRECTION

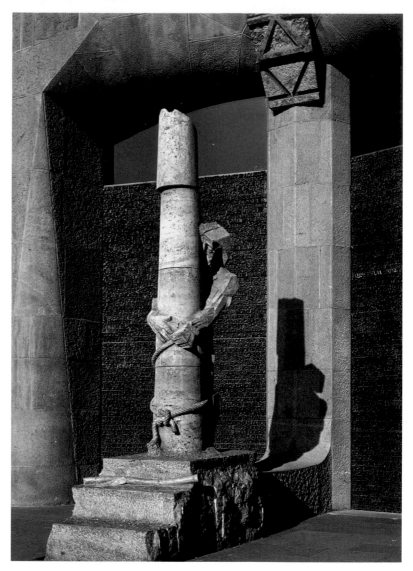

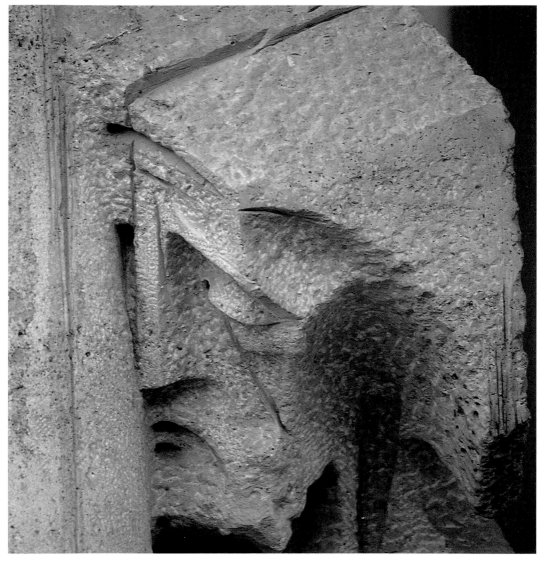

THE KNOT OF THE ROPE
SYMBOLISES PHYSICAL
MARTYRDOM, WHILE THE
REED SYMBOLISES RIDICULE,
THE MORAL PUNISHMENT. ON
SMOOTHING DOWN THE STONE
(TRAVERTINE) A FOSSIL OF A
PALM FROND WAS DISCOVERED
(CHAMAEROPS HUMILIS), A
CURIOUS COINCIDENCE SINCE
THIS PLANT IS THE SYMBOL OF
MARTYRDOM AND RESURRECTION

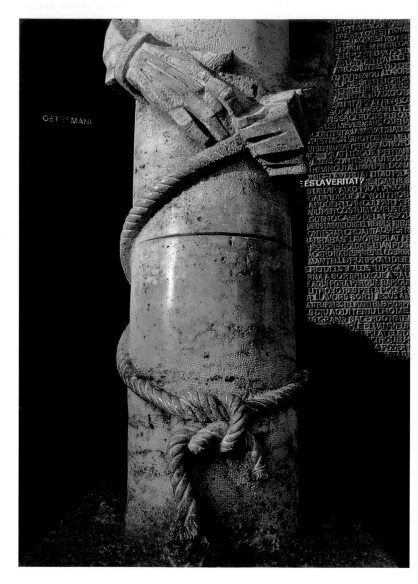

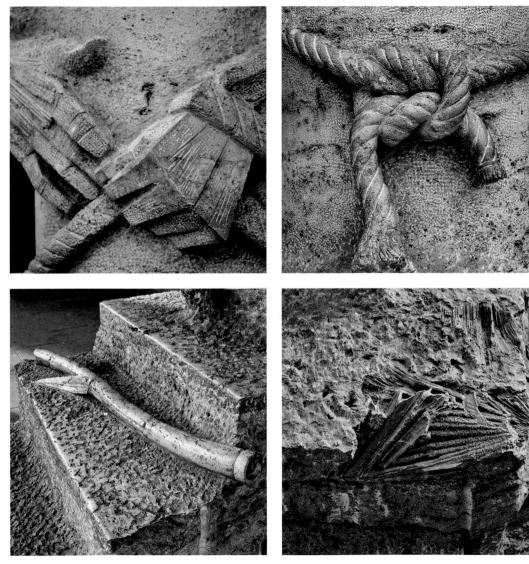

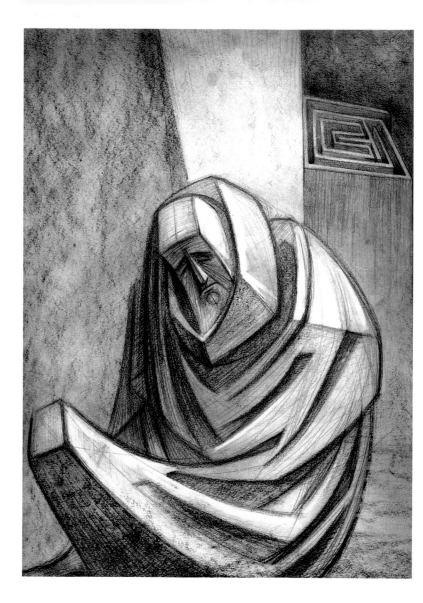

ORIGINAL DRAWING BY J. M. SUBIRACHS FOR THE FIGURE OF PETER

—

SCULPTURAL GROUP OF THE DENIAL OF PETER

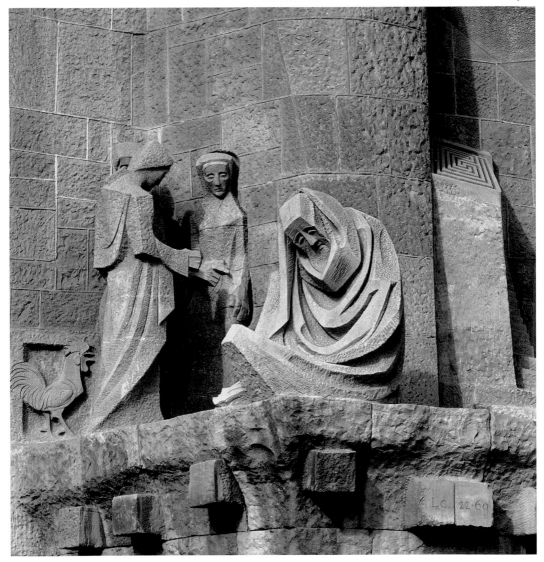

THE COCK ANNOUNCES THE
DAWN AND THE FULFILMENT
OF THE PROPHECY THAT JESUS
MADE TO PETER: "BEFORE THE
COCK CROWS YOU WILL HAVE
DENIED ME THREE TIMES"
—

THE LABYRINTH SYMBOLISES
THE PATH THAT JESUS TOOK
TO THE CROSS AND, BY
EXTENSION, THE LONELINESS
OF MAN AND THE INEXORABLE
PATH FROM LIFE TO DEATH

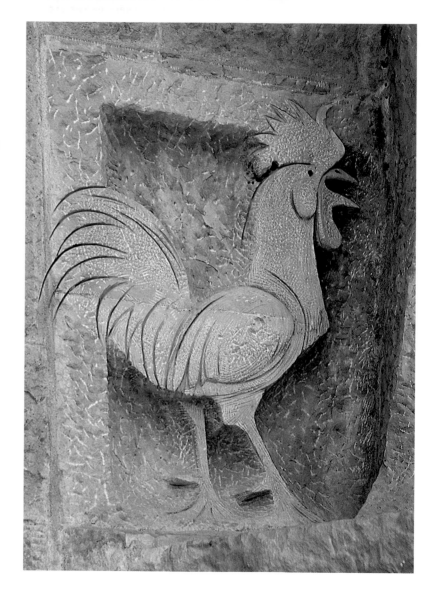

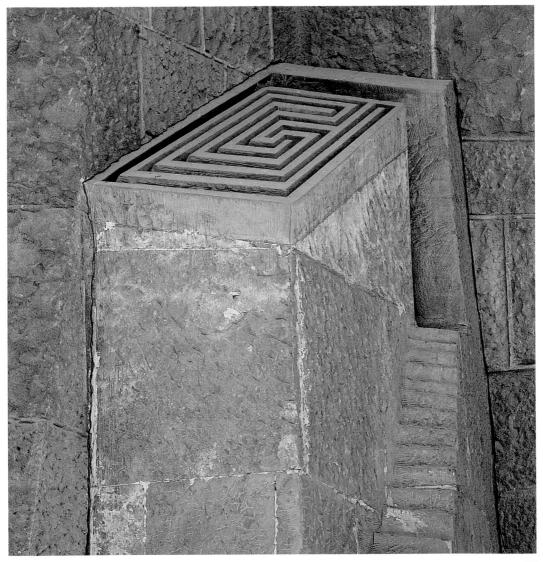

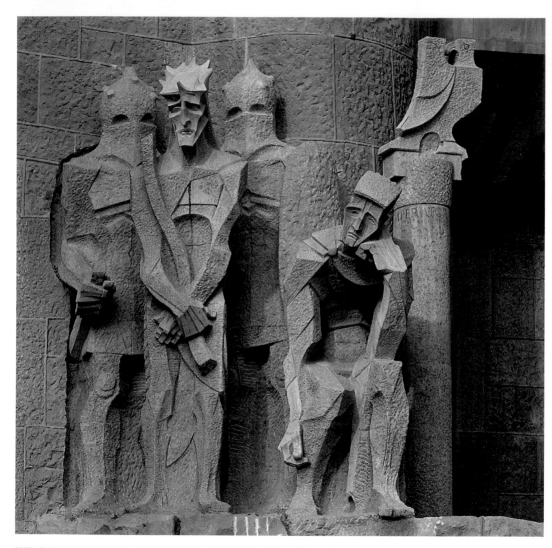

ECCE HOMO, PONTIUS PILATE AND THE ROMAN EAGLE OVER THE COLUMN WITH THE NAME OF TIBERIUS,
THE EMPEROR OF ROME AT THE TIME OF JESUS' DEATH

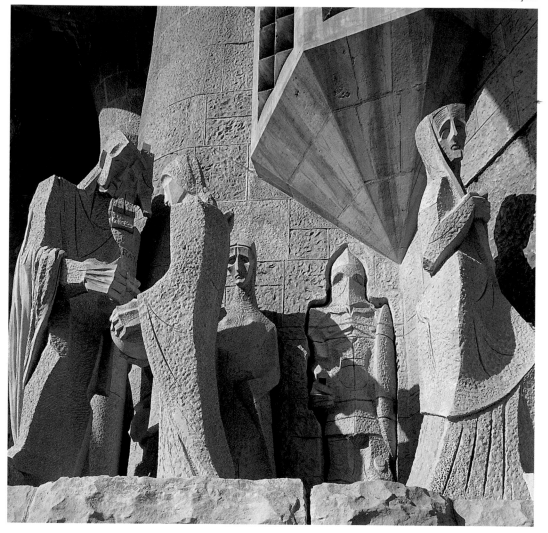

PONTIUS PILATE WASHING HIS HANDS. ON THE RIGHT HIS WIFE CLAUDIA

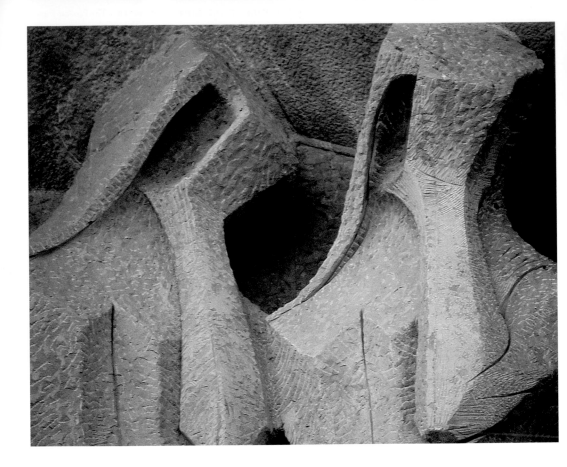

DETAIL OF THE SCULPTURAL GROUP OF THE THREE MARYS AND THE
CYRENE IN WHICH ONE CAN APPRECIATE THE DRAMATIC TENSION AND
EXPRESSIVE STRENGTH OF THESE FIGURES

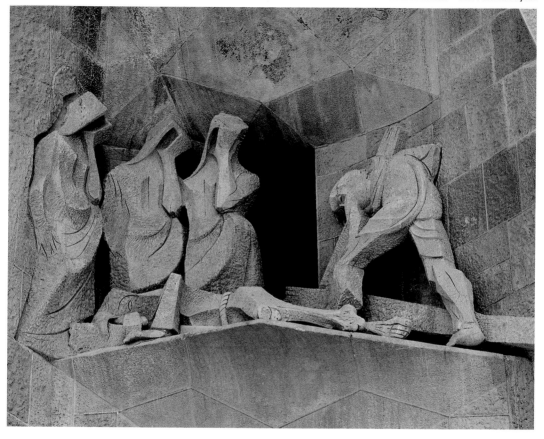

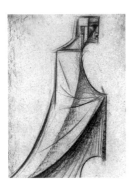

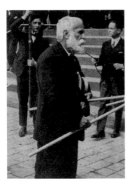

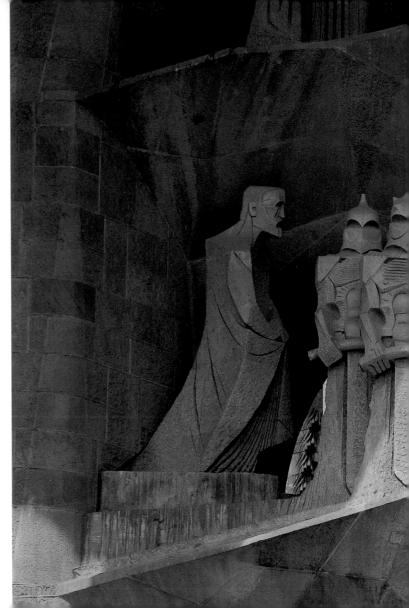

TO THE LEFT OF THIS VERONICA
GROUP, THE FIGURE OF THE
EVANGELIST NOTING DOWN
WHAT IS HAPPENING IS HOMAGE
TO GAUDÍ. THE SCULPTURE IS
INSPIRED BY A KNOWN PICTURE
OF THE ARCHITECT ON THE
EASTER PROCESSION OF 1924

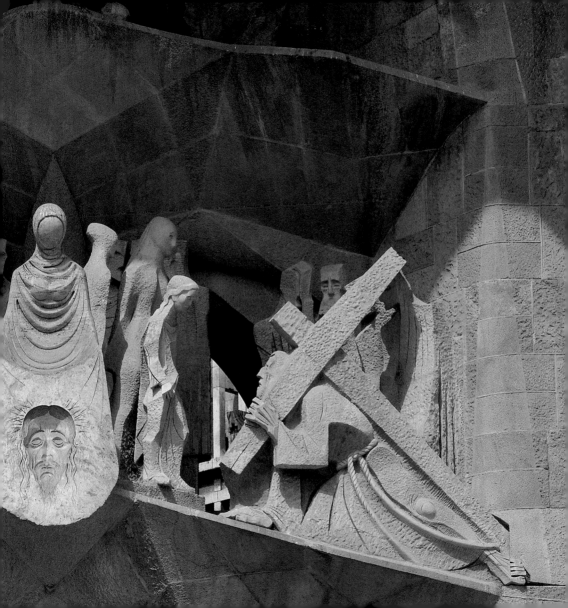

THE SCULPTURE OF
VERONICA LACKS FEATURES,
ENHANCING THE VALUE OF
THE SYMBOL AND LEGEND OF
THIS FIGURE THAT DOES NOT
APPEAR IN THE GOSPELS

—

JESUS' FACE IS SCULPTED IN
NEGATIVE TO SUGGEST THE
IMPRESSION MARKED ON THE
VEIL. SUBIRACHS THINKS THAT
THE NEGATIVE OF A FIGURE
IS LIKE THE MEMORY OF A
CHARACTER THAT IS NOT THERE
BUT WHO HAS LEFT THEIR MARK

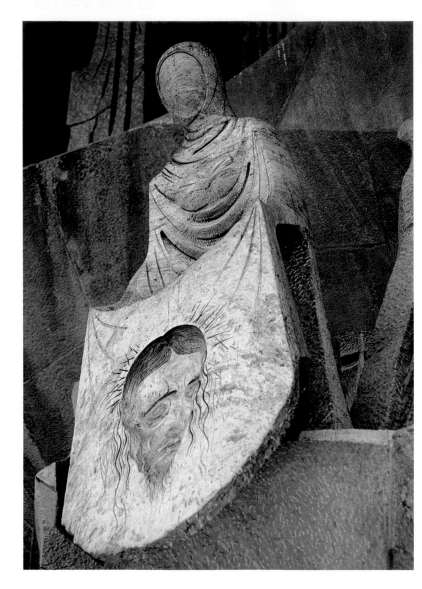

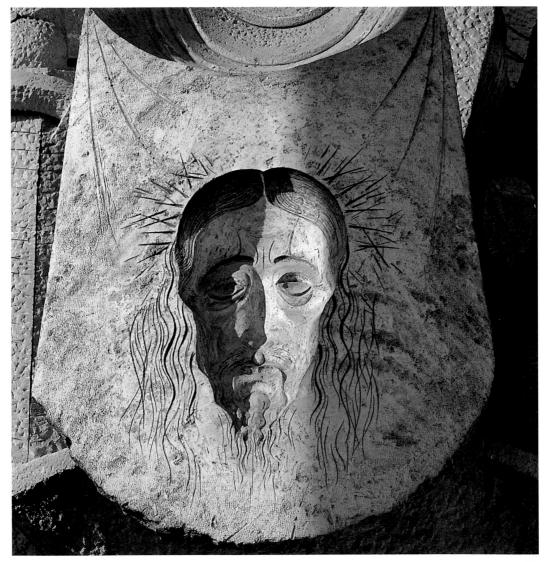

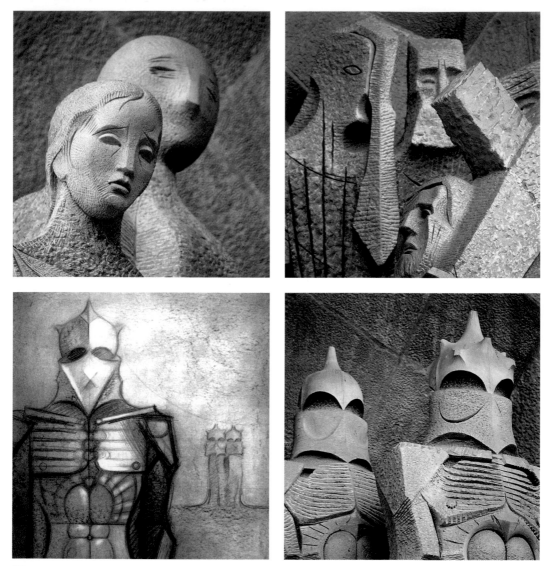

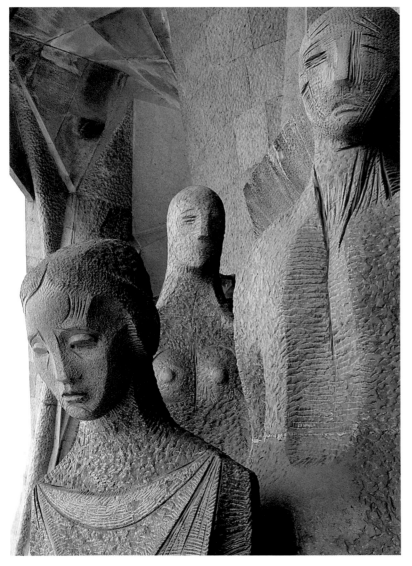

DETAILS OF THE VERONICA GROUP.
SUBIRACHS WAS INSPIRED
BY THE CHIMNEYS OF THE
PEDRERA BUILDING TO CREATE
THE WARRIORS' HELMETS

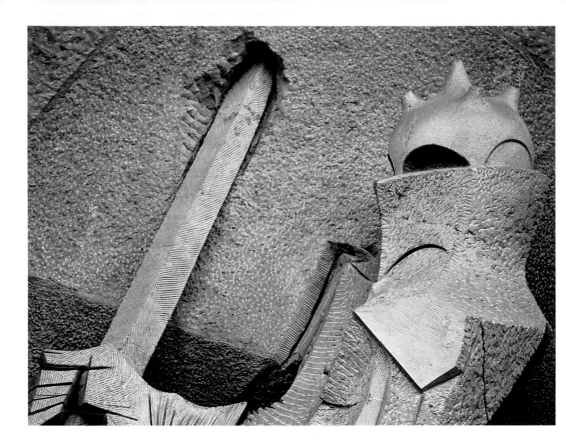

THE CENTURION LONGINUS PASSES HIS SWORD THROUGH THE SIDE OF THE CRUCIFIED JESUS

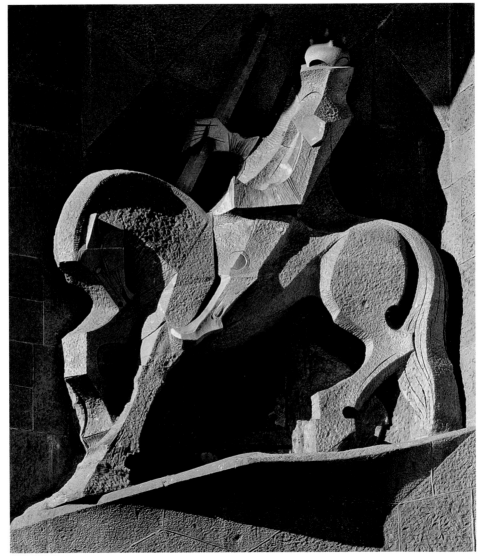

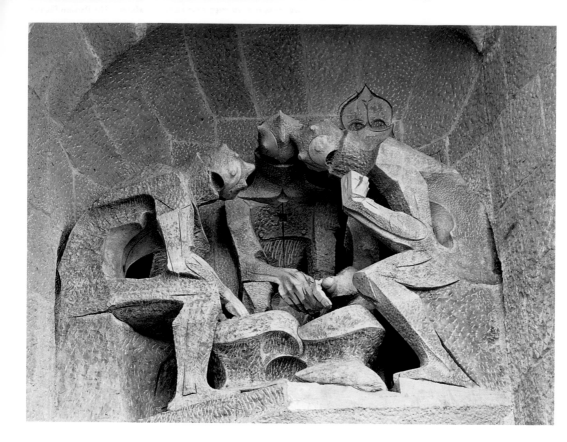

SOLDIERS PLAYING DICE FOR JESUS' ROBE
—

THE CRUCIFIED CHRIST IS THE LARGEST SCULPTURE ON THE FAÇADE
BEING 5 METRES HIGH. THIS REPRESENTATION OF THE CRUCIFIXION
BREAKS WITH TRADITIONAL ICONOGRAPHY INASMUCH AS, SURPRISINGLY,
WE ARE SHOWN A CHRIST HANGING FROM A HORIZONTAL CROSS, IN SUCH
A WAY AS HIS BODY HANGS IN SPACE, AS IF IT WERE ABOUT TO COLLAPSE
OVER THE SPECTATOR

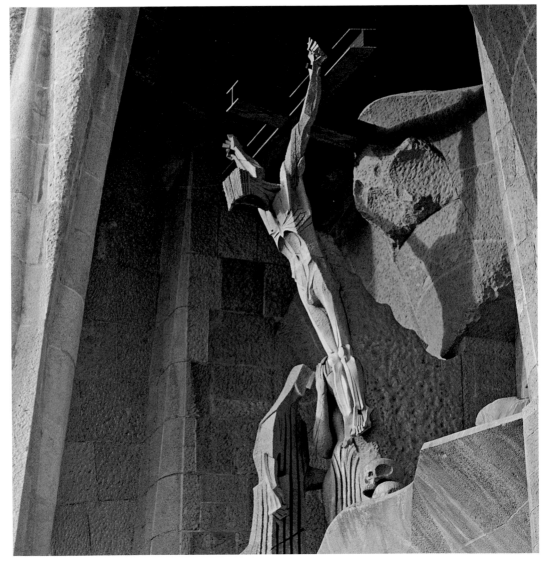

THE SKULL, PLACED AT THE
FEET OF THE CRUCIFIXION, IS
A REPRESENTATION OF THE
HEBREW WORD "GOLGOTHA",
WHICH MEANS THE PLACE OF
THE SKULL. IN THE UPPER PART,
THE WIDE VEIL OF THE TEMPLE
—

JOSEPH OF ARIMATHEA SUPPORTS
THE BODY OF JESUS WHILE
NICODEMUS -WHO BEARS A
REMARKABLE LIKENESS TO
THE SCULPTOR- ANOINTS HIM
WITH MYRRH AND ALOE

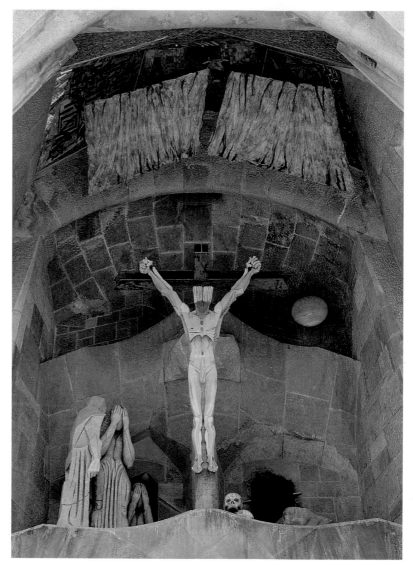

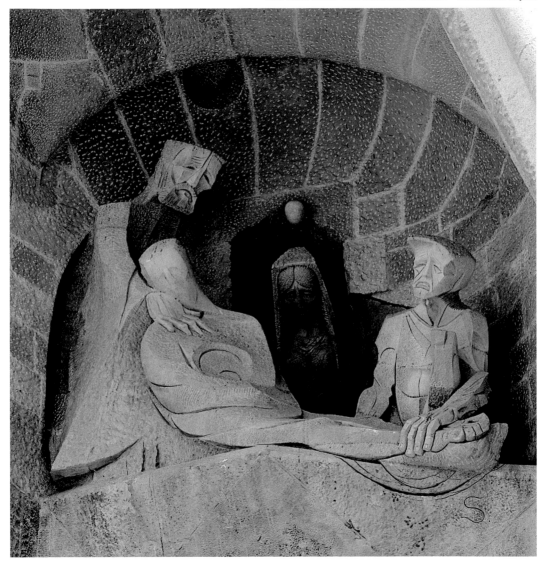

LOCATED ON THE LEFT OF THE
PASSION FAÇADE, THIS BRONZE
DOOR REPRODUCES THE NIGHT-
TIME PRAYER OF JESUS ON
THE MOUNT OF GETHSEMANE

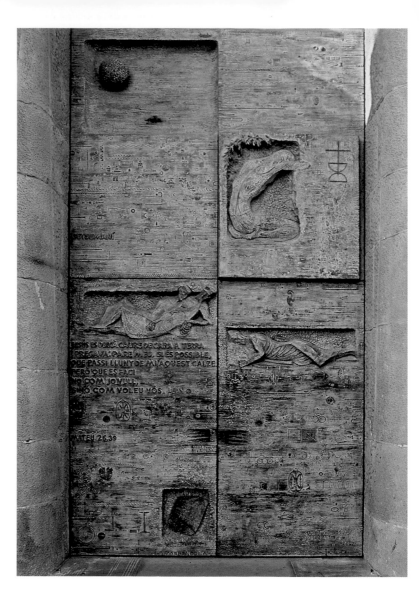

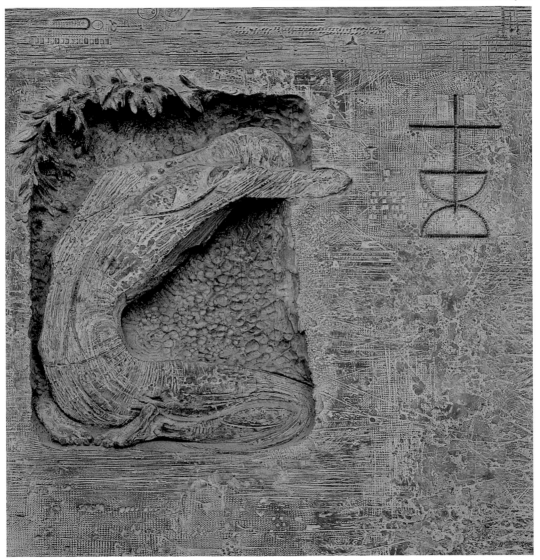

THE CENTRAL BRONZE DOORS
CONTAIN TEXTS FROM THE
GOSPELS REPRESENTED IN THE
SCULPTURES ON THE PASSION
FAÇADE. THE DOORS, SEPARATED
BY A MULLION, CONTAIN A
MAGNIFICENT TYPOGRAPHIC
MOULDING MADE UP OF 8,500
LETTERS. FOR THE SCULPTOR
SUBIRACHS THESE DOORS "ARE
LIKE TWO HUGE OPEN BOOKS THAT
WILL NOT DISTRACT WITH FIGURES
THE LONELINESS THAT THE
FIGURE OF CHRIST MUST HAVE,
TIED TO THE COLUMN IN FRONT"

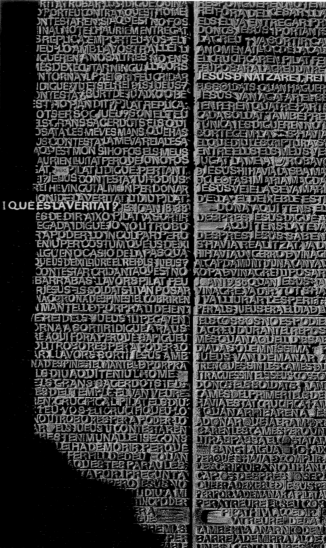

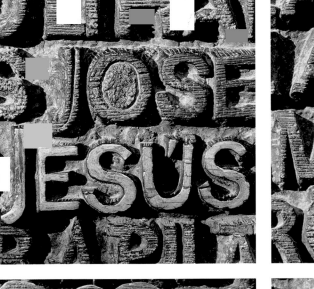

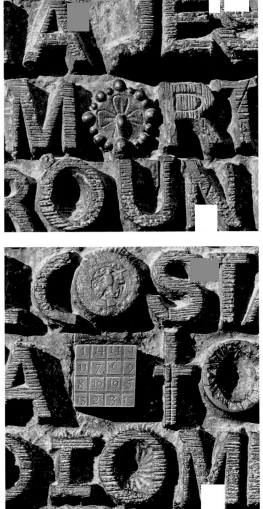

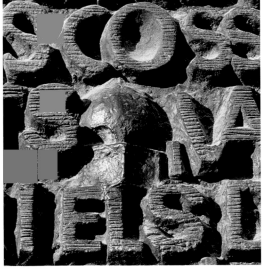

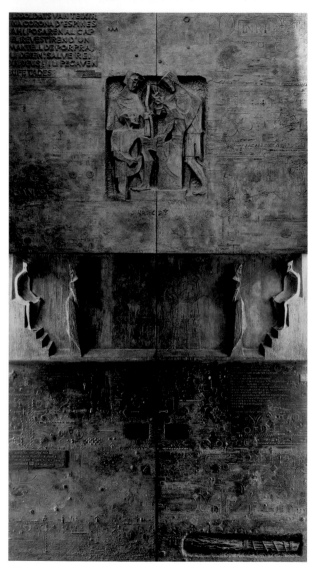

Sepharad by Salvador Espriu

Sometimes it is necessary
that a man dies for a people,
but a whole people should never die
for a single man:
always remember this, Sephared.
Make the bridges of dialogue strong
and try to understand and love
the different views and languages of your children.
Let the rain fall down slowly on the fields
and the air pass like an open hand
soft and good over the vast land.
Let Sephared live forever
in order and peace, in work,
and in the difficult and well-deserved
freedom.

Paradise XXVIII 52-51 by Dante

Hence, if in this wondrous and angelic temple,
That hath for confine only light and love,
My wish may have completion I must know

THIS DOOR, ON THE RIGHT OF THE FAÇADE,
TELLS OF THE CROWN OF THORNS AND THE
EVENTS FEATURING HEROD AND PONTIUS
PILATE. ON THE UPPER SECTION, JESUS, WITH
THE CROWN OF THORNS, IS GIVEN A REED AS A
SCEPTRE WHILE BEING BEATEN AND RIDICULED.
IN THE CENTRAL PART, LIKE A PLAY OF MIRRORS,
JESUS APPEARS ON THE LEFT BEFORE HEROD
AND ON THE RIGHT BEFORE PONTIUS PILATE.
THE LOWER PART OF THE DOOR FEATURES THE
POEMS OF SALVADOR ESPRIU AND DANTE. THE
BACKGROUND PARTS OF THE DOOR ARE FULL
OF SMALL INSET ELEMENTS THAT SUGGEST THE
PASSING OF TIME

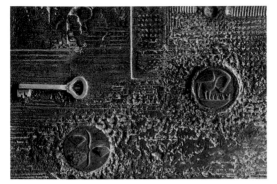

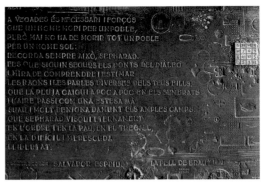

A VEGADES ÉS NECESSARI I FORÇÓS
QUE UN HOME MORI PER UN POBLE,
PERÒ MAI NO HA DE MORIR TOT UN POBLE
PER UN HOME SOL:
RECORDA SEMPRE AIXÒ, SEPHARAD.
FES QUE SIGUIN SEGURS ELS PONTS DEL DIÀLEG
I MIRA DE COMPRENDRE I ESTIMAR
LES RAONS I LES PARLES DIVERSES DELS TEUS FILLS,
QUE LA PLUJA CAIGUI A POC A POC EN ELS SEMBRATS
I L'AIRE PASSI COM UNA ESTESA MÀ
SUAU I MOLT BENIGNA DAMUNT ELS AMPLES CAMPS.
QUE SEPHARAD VISQUI ETERNAMENT
EN L'ORDRE I EN LA PAU, EN EL TREBALL,
EN LA DIFÍCIL I MERESCUDA
LLIBERTAT.
SALVADOR ESPRIU   LA PELL DE BRAU LIII

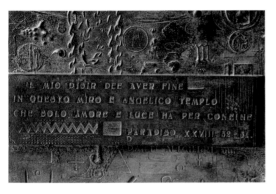

IL MIO DISIR DEE AVER FINE
IN QUESTO MIRO E ANGELICO TEMPLO
CHE SOLO AMORE E LUCE HA PER CONFINE
PARADISO XXVIII 52-54

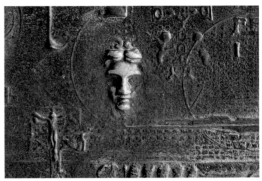

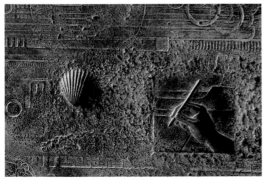

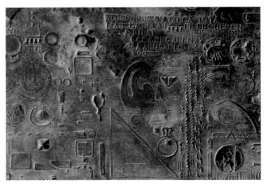

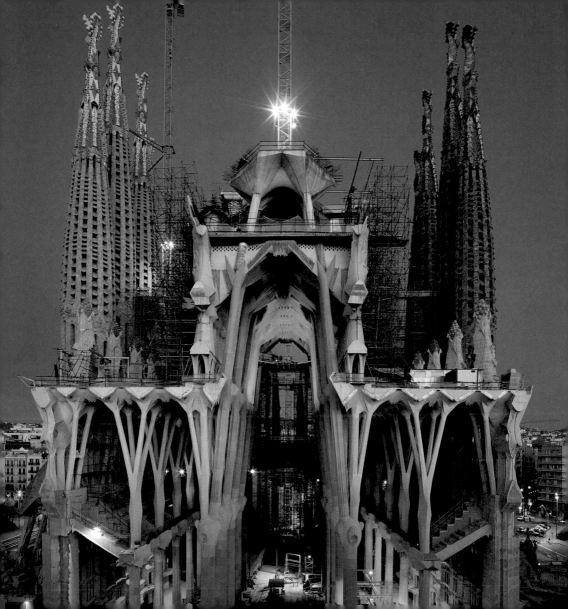

The Glory Façade

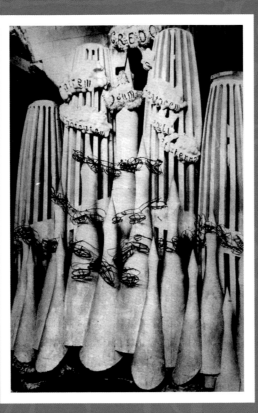

ORIGINAL MODEL OF THE GLORY FAÇADE

←

STATE OF THE WORKS (2003)

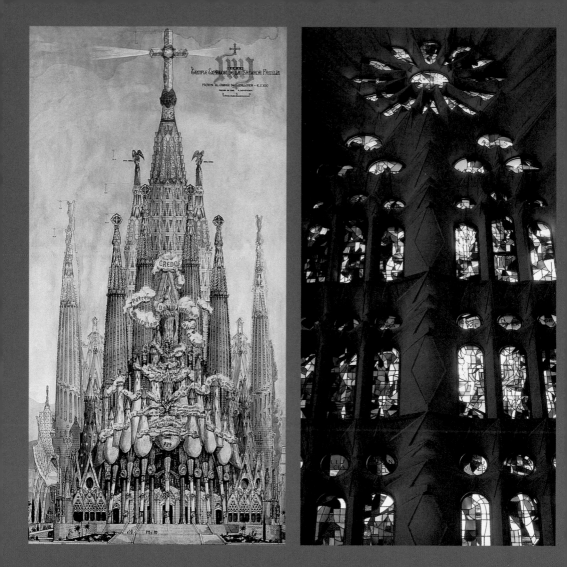

DRAWING BY RAMÓN BERENGUER OF THE GLORY FAÇADE | STAINED-GLASS WINDOW OF THE SIDE NAVE

The Glory Façade

A wide bridge over Carrer Mallorca will give access to the Glory Façade, the largest and most spectacular "front" of the whole building with its four towers, much taller than those of the Nativity and Passion Façades.

Gaudí used to say that the Glory Façade would spell out the last events: the Death, Judgment, descent into Hell and then Glory. Indeed, when one arrives in front of the great portal, the first thing to see, in the ground, is Death, "Death is in the tombs at the entrance." And he also said: "On the highest point [of this entrance] is God the Father; under it, the great rose window of the Holy Spirit, and under that, Jesus, with the instruments of the Passion, judging Men." In other words, this entrance was also to be the symbolic place of judgment, after which sinners go to Hell or to Glory. It is precisely in the basement of this part of the church (where the museum is now) that Gaudí wanted to create a representation of the condemnation of different types of sinners. From certain indications by Gaudí we know that Hell would have been depicted from the outside, looking through barred windows, and its style would have been between Expressionism and popular art.

From a certain distance, we can imagine this façade, multicoloured of course like the rest, but brighter, as suggested in certain paintings that have come down to us. Five doorways, as well as two at the ends, will give access to the interior. Over these seven doors, there are to be large, coloured clouds, which at the same time are enormous tears hanging from the upper part of the façade. These are undoubtedly a symbol of expiation, since the church is expiatory. Above that will be the towers, higher than anything constructed so far. And the domes of the four gospel writers Matthew, Mark, Luke and John, will soar higher still, and rise straight out of the roof of the church. In the midst of these four domes will be that of Jesus Christ, which will rise to the impressive height of 170 metres (550 feet). In the background, above the apse, will be the dome of the Virgin, a little less high.

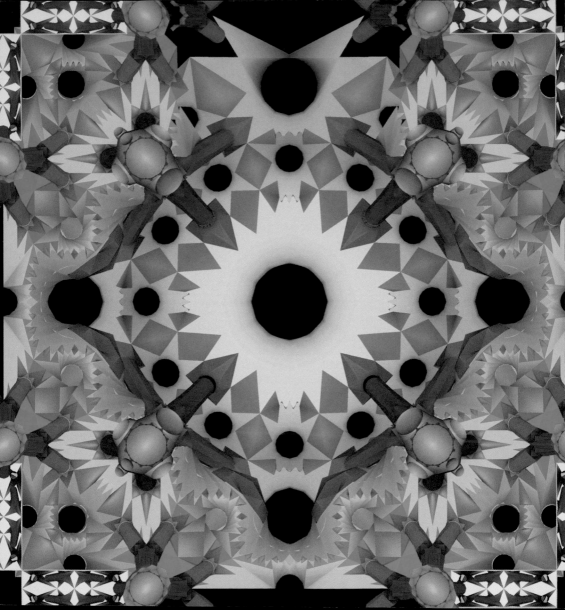

Interior of the temple

These spectacular exterior volumes will be in harmony with the interior ones. The temple is a basilica of five naves, the central one being the highest, to which correspond five doorways on the Glory Façade, as well as two side doors that lead to the Penitence and Baptistery chapels. The model of the sacristy will be used to plan the cupola of the Virgin.

At the far end of the central nave will be the main altar, surrounded by the apse with its stained glass windows. It is here that the great religious services are to be celebrated, and for which Gaudí made a number of studies over several years –the latter serving as general models for the entire cathedral. If the façades have, as has been seen, multiple symbolism, the same could be said of the temple ground plan, since every door, every column, almost every space will have its specific or symbolic reference to, for example, each of the Catalan diocese and Spanish archdiocese, to each Church of Hispanic America and to each of the five continents, to the apostles, to the great founders of orders and to outstanding saints, to the theological virtues and to the sacraments, and a long etcetera, to act as both a reminder and location finder.

At the present time it is already possible to admire the straight or slightly inclined pillars –unusually furrowed or striated as if the material had been pulled or twisted. The tops of these columns sprout branches, so that each column supports the roof at various points. This space has been built thanks to the new technologies in calculus and to computerised drawings undertaken by the Temple's technical office and by the universities of Victoria (New Zealand), Deakin and Royal Melbourne Institute of Technology (Australia) and the Polytechnic of Catalonia. The structural whole, as Gaudí wished, resembles a wood, a symbolic and yet almost real wood –with the stone roof poised above it. A confluence, no less, of prodigious Gaudian art and the most sophisticated technology.

COMPUTERISED REPRESENTATION OF THE TRANSEPT VAULTING

In closing, let us return to the Nativity Façade, but on the inside, constructed by Gaudí. Here the different levels of the interior can now be seen, thanks to the doors and windows which open onto it. These are reached, or will be reached, by stairs. Where the rose window is, for example, we can make out the floors of the galleries known as *cantorías* or chantries. These are where the singers will sit protected by rails, facing the altar during the great festivals of the church. At which time, in Gaudí's fertile and optimistic imagination there will be gathered together dozens of priests and thousands of choristers and worshippers.

Although the arch, the rose window and the large window are clearly Gothic in style, Gaudí has introduced new volumes and shapes. We can already see the geometry that will evolve into the stylised geometric shapes of the towers –particularly evident in the balconies, floors, entrances to passages and the cube shapes on little columns.

It should be remembered that Gaudí from his elegant youth to his lucid but painful old age, with a tense middle-age in between, had many labourers and workmen, many foremen and craftsmen working for him. These he knew how to train and to orchestrate with consummate mastery, along with the mathematicians, engineers, photographers and sculptors who worked together on what was a complex, innovative task.

He was assisted by architects Berenguer, Rubió, Jujol, Canaleta and Ràfols, and in the last stage, by Sugrañes and Quintana; these last continued with the work after his death in 1926, until the towers of the Nativity Façade were completed. After the Civil War, the Directors of Works were Quintana, Puig i Boada and Bonet Garí with help from Bergós, Martinell and Dapena, and, in more recent decades, Cardoner and Bonet Armengol. The latter, along with the architects Margarit, Buxadé and Gómez, has been responsible for the construction from Gaudí's original plaster model of the main nave.

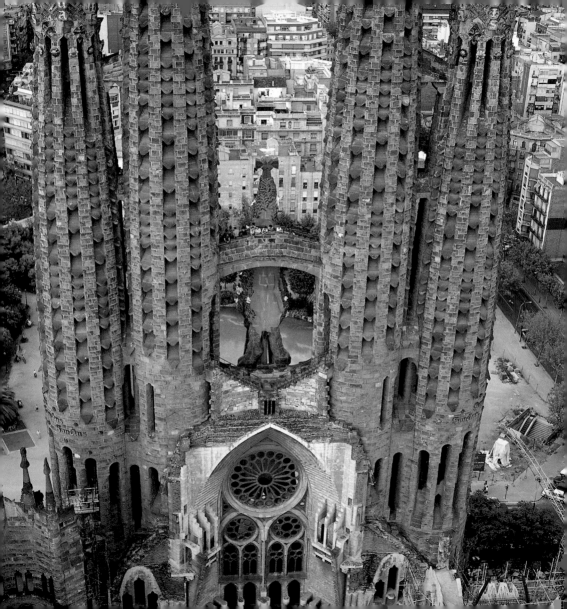

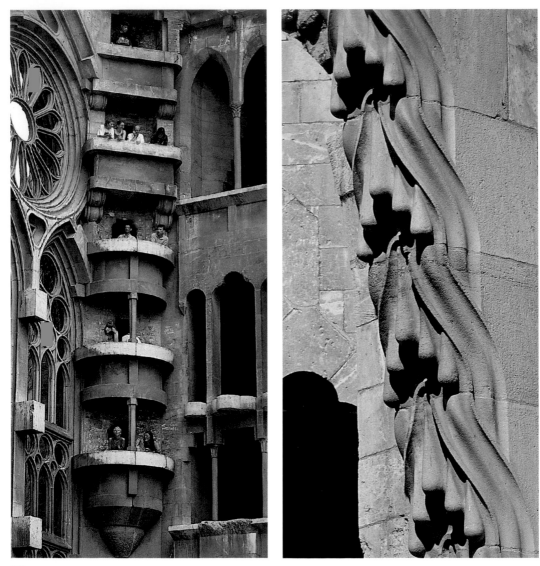

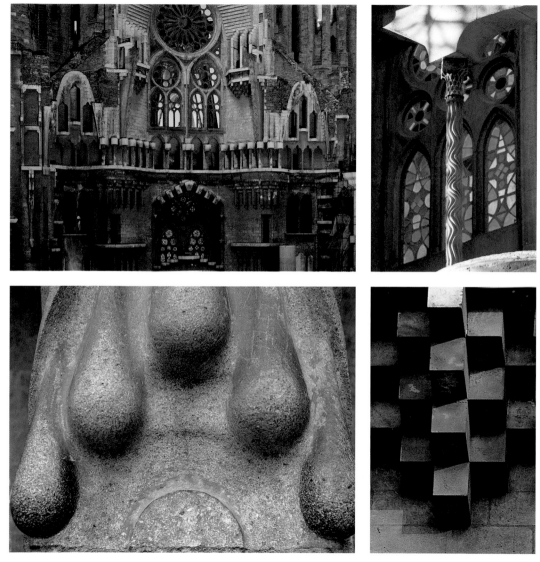

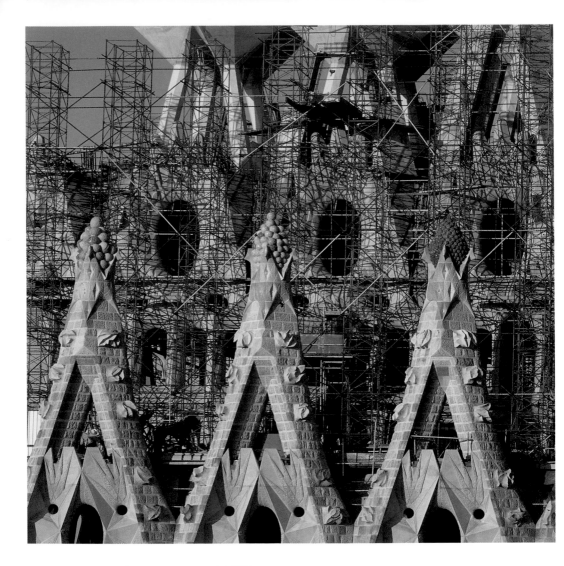

SIDE FAÇADE OF THE NAVE │ AERIAL VIEW OF THE WORKS (2004)

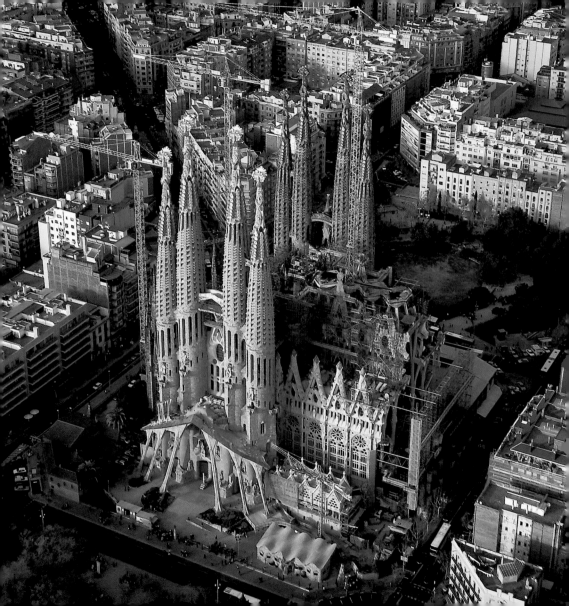

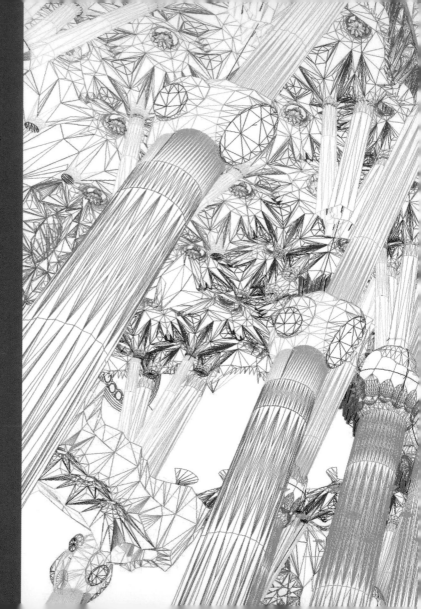

COMPUTERISED STUDY OF THE
INTERIOR OF THE TEMPLE NAVES

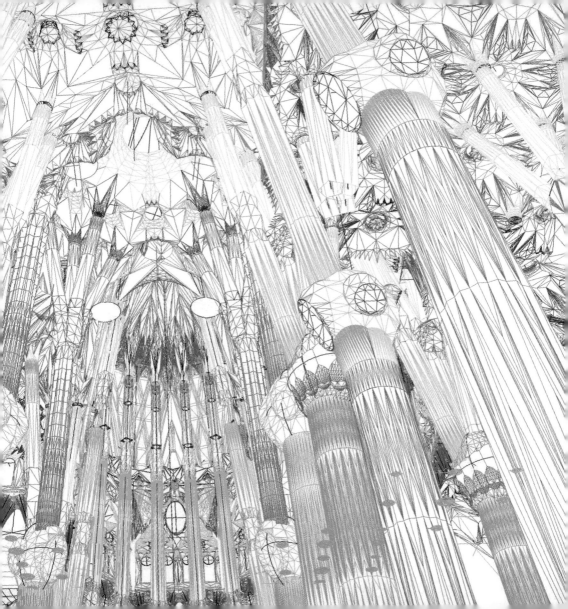

ARBOREAL COLUMNS
—

FAÇADE OF THE SIDE NAVE

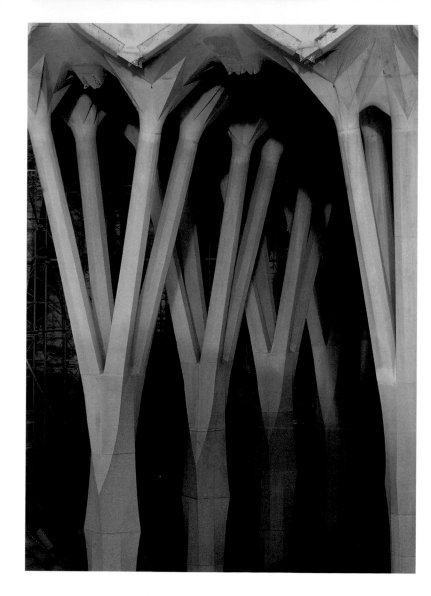

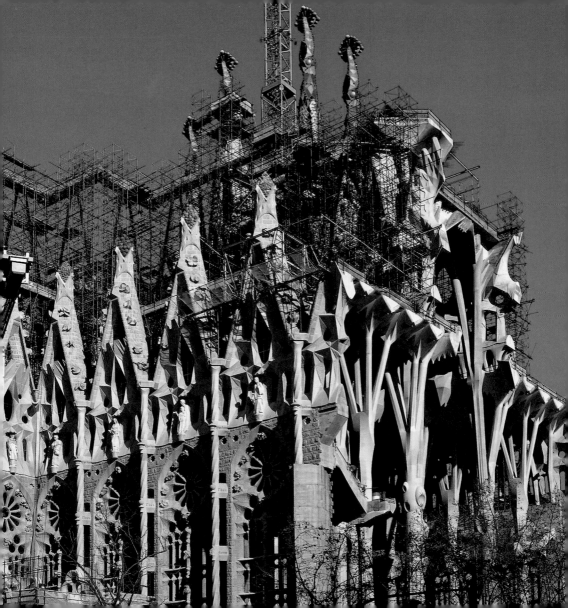

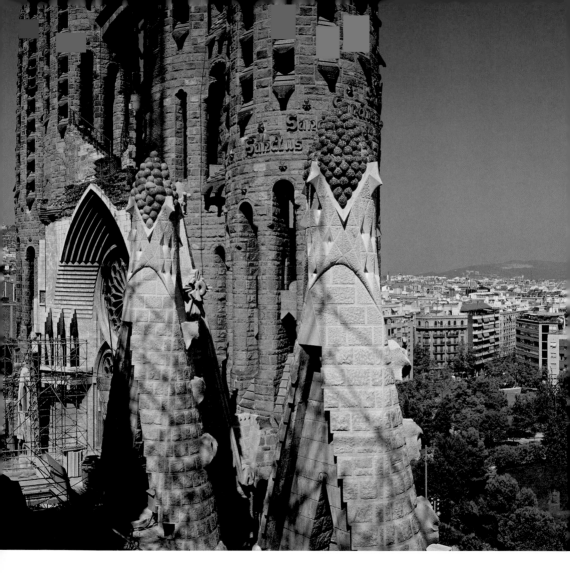

THE FRUIT CROWNING THE PINNACLES OF THE SIDE NAVE, PRODUCED BY E. SOTOO, SYMBOLISES GOOD WORKS

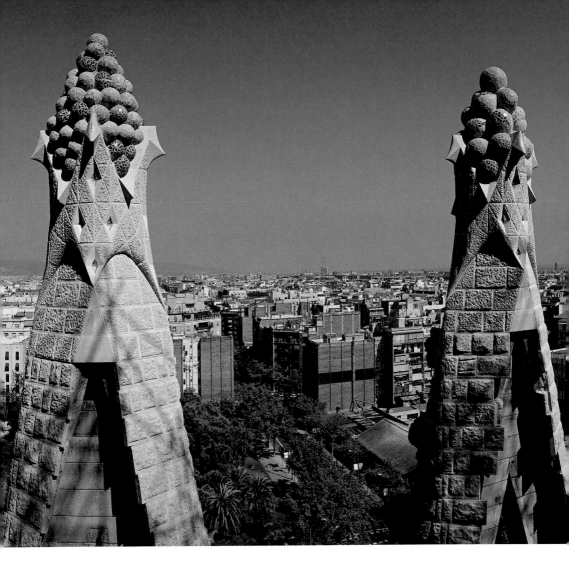

THE COLUMNS ARE MADE FROM
MATERIALS OF DIFFERING
RESISTANCE. THE THICKEST
AND MOST SOLID ARE OF RED
PORPHYRY; THE DARK ONES,
SECOND IN RESISTANCE, OF
BASALT; THE LIGHTER ONES
OF GRANITE AND, FINALLY, THE
COLUMNS BELOW THE CHOIR
STALLS ARE STONE FROM
MONTJUÏC, THE LEAST RESISTANT
MATERIAL

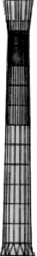
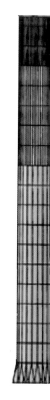
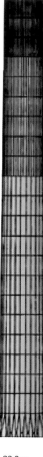

Height	11,1 m	14,8 m	18,5 m	22,2 m
Diameter	1,05 m	1,4 m	1,75 m	2,1 m
Base	hexagon	octagon	decagon	dodecagon
Material	Montjuïc stone	granite	basalt	porphyry

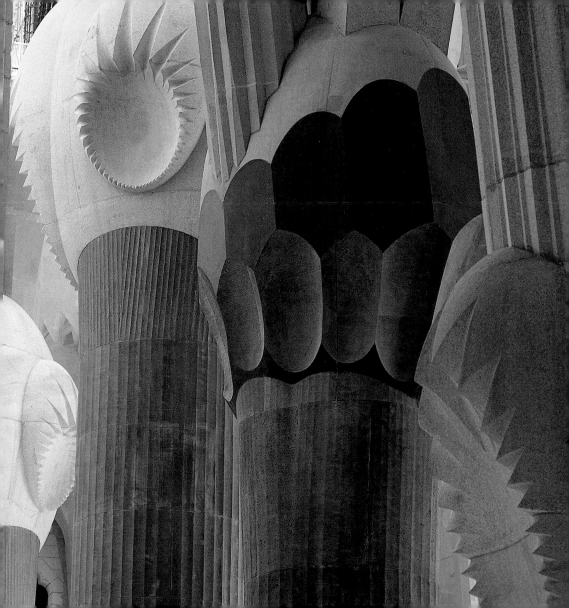

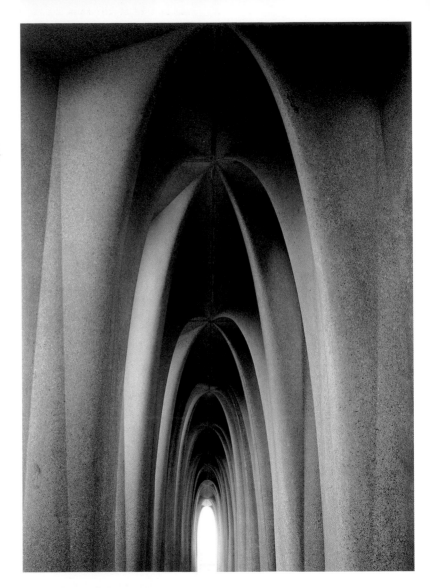

TRIFORIUM GALLERY OF THE
CENTRAL NAVE, DETAIL OF THE
INTERIOR OF THE LATERAL NAVE
AND THE UPPER PART OF ONE OF
THE GRANITE KNOTS

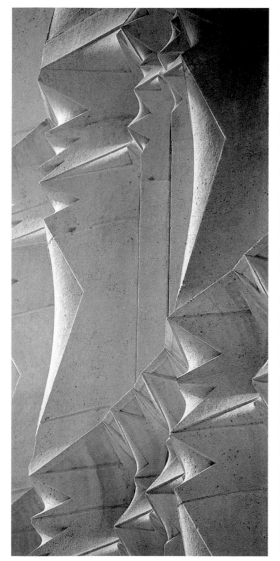

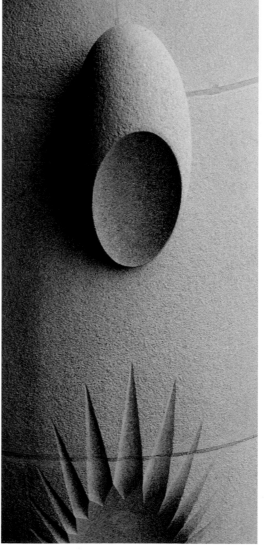

GAUDÍ WANTED THE TEMPLE TO
BE SUPPORTED OVER A SYSTEM
OF COLUMNS THAT IMITATED THE
FORM AND STRUCTURE OF THE
TREE. IN THIS WAY THE NAVES
ARE LIKE A FOREST IN WHICH THE
COLUMNS ARE THE TRUNKS WITH
BRANCHES AND THE VAULTING
THE FOLIAGE, THROUGH WHICH
PENETRATE THE SUNRAYS

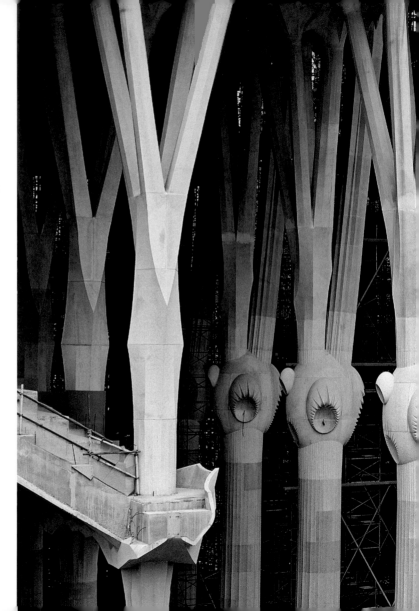

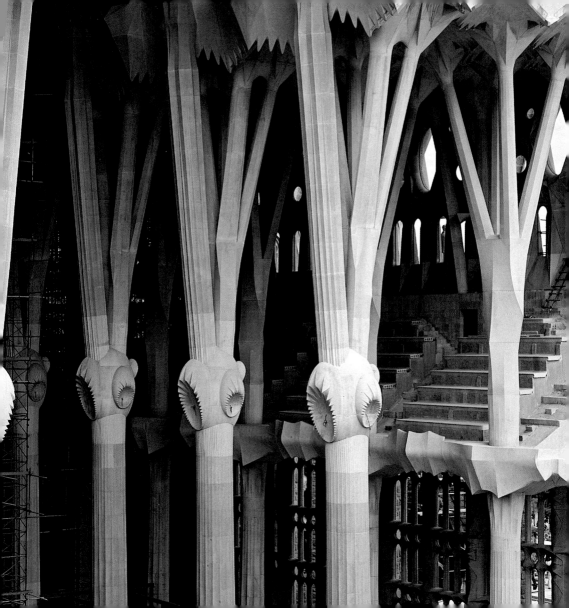

THE KNOTS ARE THE
INTERMEDIATE ELEMENTS
BETWEEN THE COLUMNS AND
THE VAULTING, THE TRUNK AND
THE BRANCHES. THE CREATION
OF THESE PIECES IS BASED ON
A COMPLEX SYSTEM OF FUSION
OF ELLIPSOIDS. THE ARCHITECT
WANTED TO USE SOME OF THESE
KNOTS TO PLACE THE LIGHTING
ELEMENTS FOR THE INTERIOR OF
THE NAVES

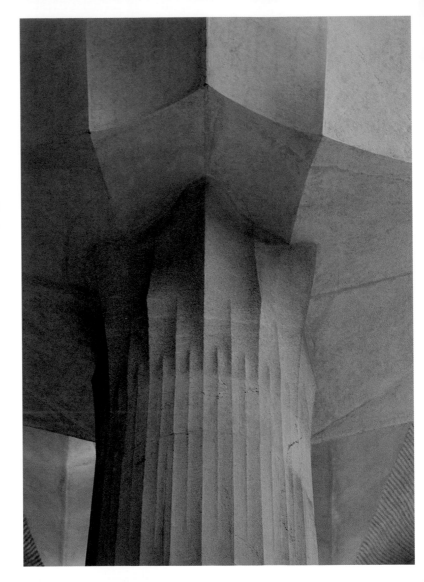

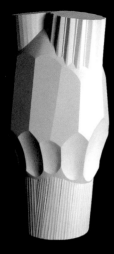

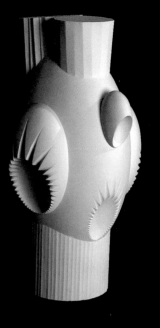

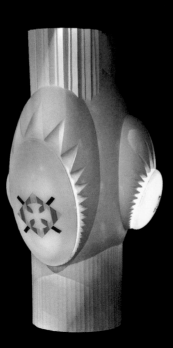

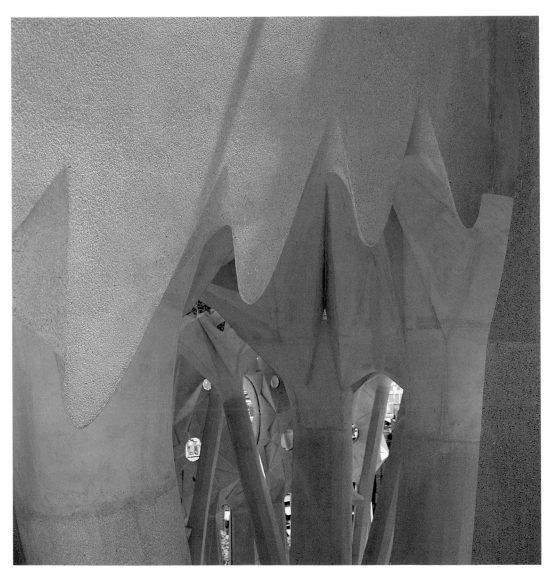

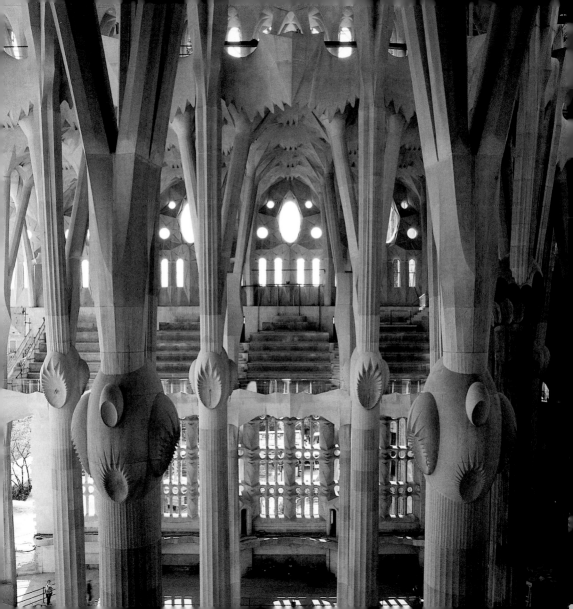

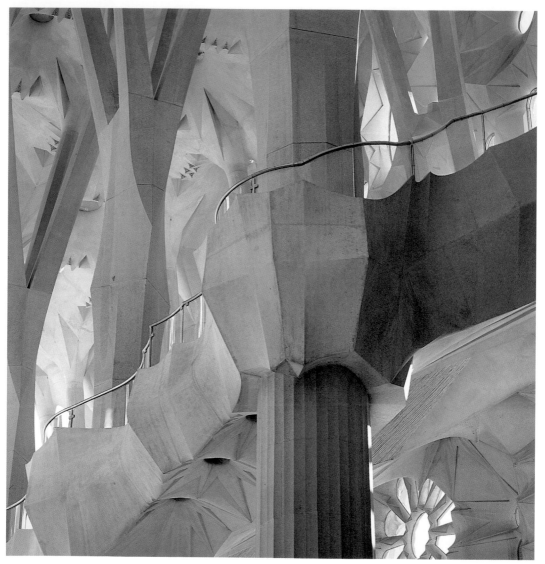

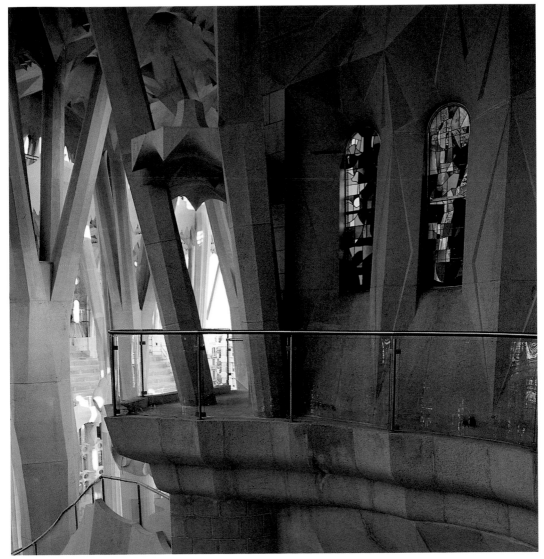

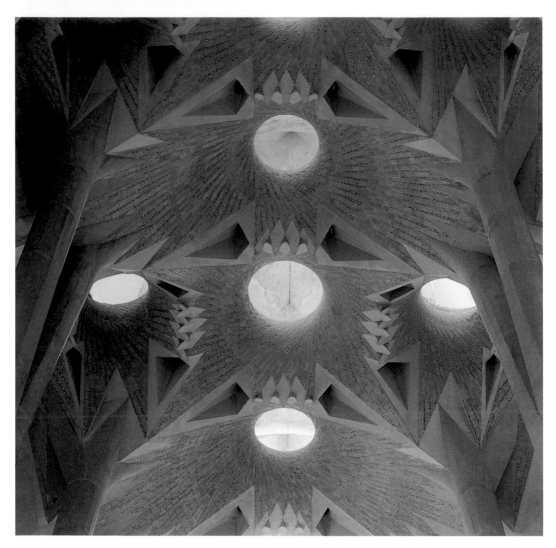

VAULTING OF THE CENTRAL NAVE AT 45 METRES HEIGHT. THE HYPERBOLIC VAULTING COLLECTS AND DISTRIBUTES THE LIGHT, JUST AS GAUDÍ WANTED. SIMULATING THE LEAVES OF THE TREES, SOME ENDS OF THE VAULTING ARE COVERED IN VENETIAN MOSAIC

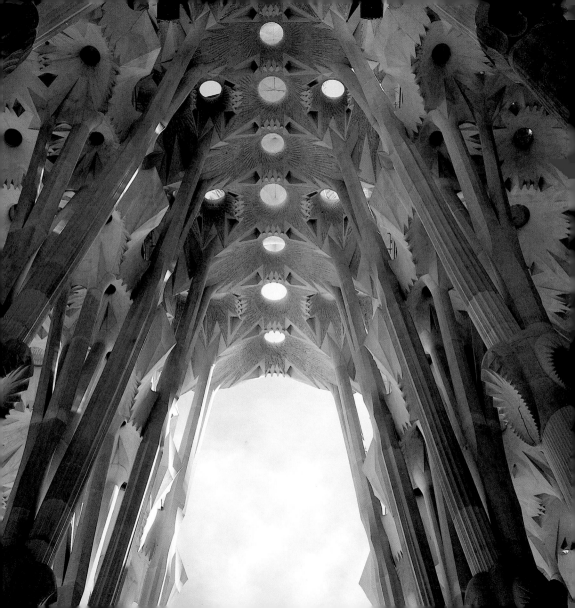

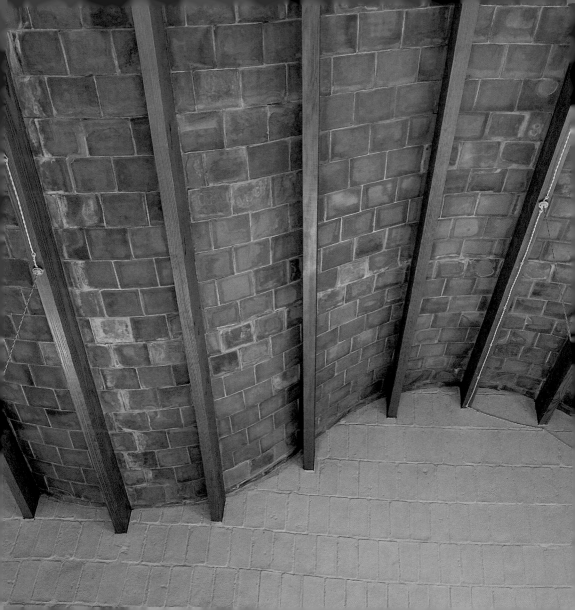

The Schools

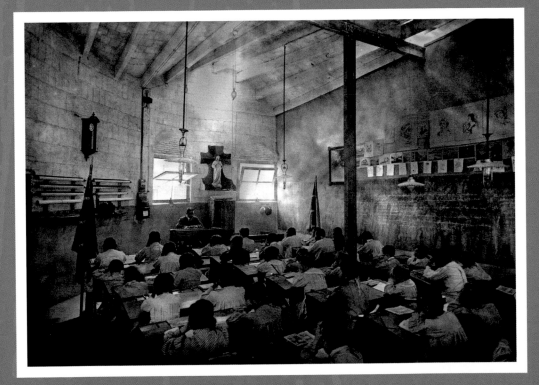

CLASS INSIDE THE SCHOOLS

←
DETAIL OF THE INTERIOR OF THE
UNDULATING ROOF

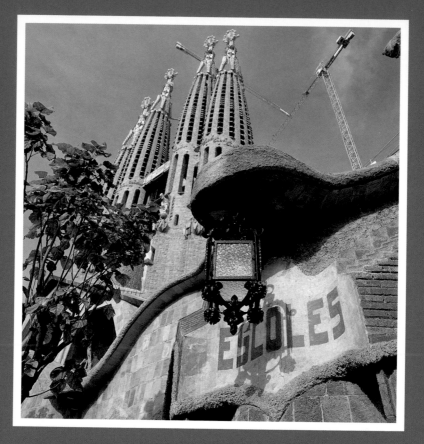

ENTRANCE TO THE SCHOOLS AT THE FOOT OF THE PASSION FAÇADE

The Schools

Like a midget next to an elephant, the schools building is dwarfed by the Sagrada Familia. There have been commentators –Le Corbusier for example– who have said that this modest little pavilion is more brilliant than the arrogant, mystic skyscraper. Built with simple brick, almost free of decoration, there is marvellous movement here, and a roof that is simpler and more complex than anything ever seen before, an interplay of swaying waves. And this is nothing more, or less, than a nursery school.

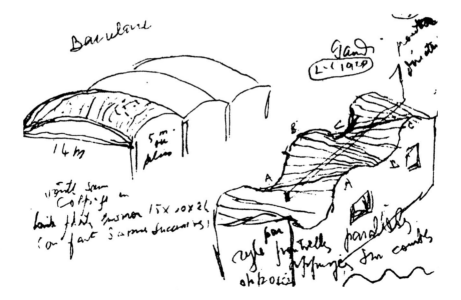

DRAWING OF THE SCHOOL BY LE CORBUSIER IN 1928

DETAIL OF THE ROOF.
ILLUSTRATION BY J. BERGÓS
—

THE UNDULATING FORMS OF THE
ROOF PROVIDE STRUCTURAL
RESISTANCE FOR THE BUILDING

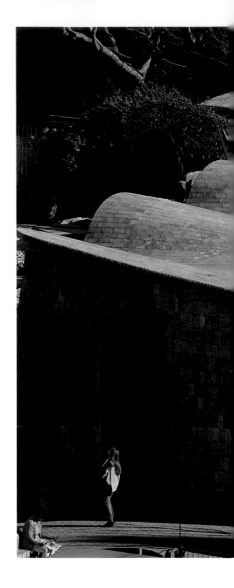

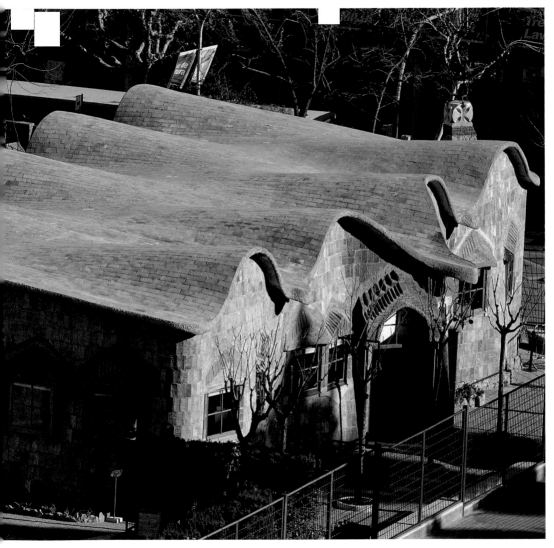

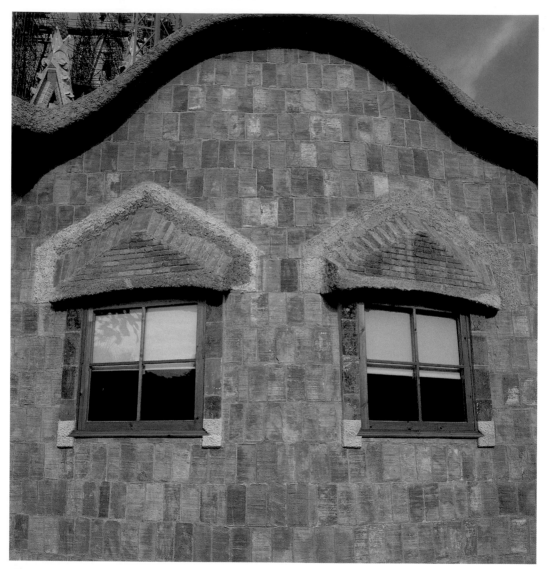

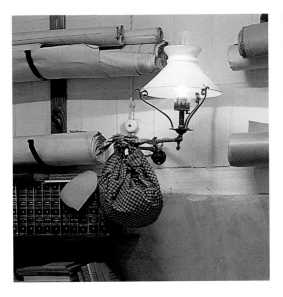

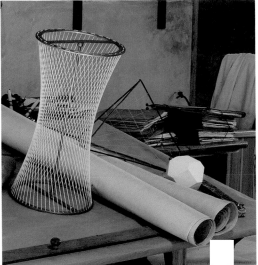

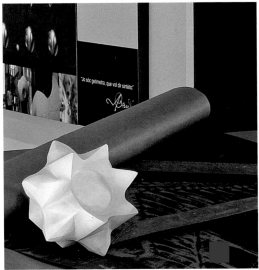

DETAIL OF THE FAÇADE OF THE SCHOOLS

RECREATION OF GAUDÍ'S STUDIO IN THE SAGRADA FAMILIA

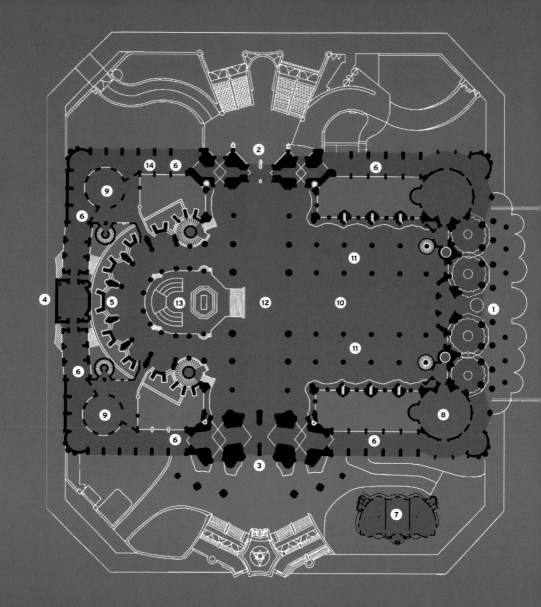